Tangled Roots

Eunice Long

authorHOUSE®

AuthorHouse™
1663 Liberty Drive
Bloomington, IN 47403
www.authorhouse.com
Phone: 1-800-839-8640

First published by AuthorHouse 8/27/2009

ISBN: 978-1-4490-1621-0 (e)
ISBN: 978-1-4490-1620-3 (sc)

Printed in the United States of America
Bloomington, Indiana

This book is printed on acid-free paper.

Dedication

I dedicate this book to my husband Bill, who has been most patient, considerate, and kind. Bill supported me in all directions, and held my hand all the way home. I must also include my daughter Linda, who encouraged me with her positive attitude and loving care. She kept pushing me in the right direction. "You can do it. I know you can." To my son Eddie, a huge thank you. He was much help in making decisions, typing, and the photography work. Without his computer expertise, I would have been lagging far behind. Also to my granddaughters, Brandi and Shellee, thank you for your support and loving care.

Tangled Roots

Marcia was a frail and weak child, yet the obligations laid upon her forced her to be a woman of limited strength. The funeral had been over less than an hour when Marcia was put to her first test of womanhood, strength and courage. She here functioned with confidence and without hesitation as Maria came running through the kitchen door with a jar full of butterflies and screaming that she was hungry. She was also very dirty and tired. Marcia held the child's face between her hands. "Your face is like ice. Do you want some hot cocoa while I fix something to eat?" Her voice was soft but a bit trembled. She kissed Maria's cheek and then went to the stove to hide her tears. The child did not speak, but kept examining her collection of butterflies. Marcia wiped her tear-streaked face with the dish towel as she placed the steaming cup before her little sister. "It's hot darling," she warned her, kissing her again. "I'll be back in a minute; I'm going to the back room to see about Paps." She found him lying prostrate across his bed sobbing bitterly. She closed his door gently and did not disturb him. "Poor Paps", she whispered to herself."He will about die without Mama."She began to cry again, holding the dish rag to her face to muffle her sobs. Remembering that Mrs. Baggett had given her a handkerchief at the cemetery, she now went into the front room and searched for it among sweaters that were piled on the bed. Not finding it, she looked on the floor around the bed, and then under it, but the handkerchief was not found. "I know I brought it home," she whispered to herself. "It was a real pretty handkerchief with lace and blue flowers." Finally, with a shrug of her shoulders, she went back to the kitchen where Maria still sit sipping her cocoa from a spoon. Her jar of butterflies was sitting on the table in front of her. Jo stood staring at the door until a light shown

The child was sniffling and Marcia rushed over to her. "Here," She said, using the dish rag on her sister's face now."Please, don't cry. We will eat something in a few minutes, then you can take a nap." "I'm not crying." Maria proclaimed."And I will not take a nap." She unscrewed the cap off her jar and inserted her chubby little fist, pulled out a white handkerchief with lace and blue flowers, and scrubbed her face with it. "See, I'm not crying." She said. Marcia observed the handkerchief and smiled. "I think you just took a little cold at the cemetery. It was very cold

and windy. Maybe Papa will give you some medicine."
"I will not take it." Maria shouted."When will Mama be
back home?" Marcia again turned her attention to the
stove. She was frying bacon, but it was now burning. The
aroma had reached the back room filling the nostrils of
Sam Marshall and bringing him to his feet. He entered
the smoke-filled kitchen just as a loud knock was placed
on the back door. He unlocked the door and let Jo, his
sister, in.

Just as he had expected and indeed hoped for, Jo was
heavily burdened with a large box filled with enough
food to last them for a couple of days. Jo re-opened the
door to let some smoke out of the kitchen. Then turning
abruptly to see what was on fire, she noticed the iron
skillet of bacon charcoals. She found a lid to cover the
skillet, and asked her brother to sit it on the back porch
to cool. She put her arms around Marcia and held her
close for a moment."Be careful my dear." she warned her.
"A grease fire can be very dangerous."

Turning now to her brother, she gave him an
affectionate slap on the back. What she actually wanted
to do was to take him into her arms as she had done
for his small daughters, in an effort to comfort him.
Being a man though, he must be treated like one less
her comforting efforts should break him."Get busy!" she
said to him. "Unpack this box and let's eat." He took the
bowls from the box and handed them to Marcia, who
placed them on the table that she had already set. She
had not set a place for herself however, for she had not
intended to eat. She felt too sad, and now that Aunt Jo
had arrived, let her do the work. After removing the covers

5

from the bowls, seeing the hot peas and butterbeans with ham hocks, she changed her mind and reached for a plate for herself and Aunt Jo. The last items taken from the box were two pones of corn-bread, that were still hot enough to warm her hands. Aunt Jo poured the milk and commanded that everyone be seated while the food was still hot. Jo looked at her brother who was pale and quiet, and noticed a slight quivering of his upper lip. "Grace the table Sam," she said, not taking her eyes off him. His face fell forward as if bowing for prayer, but from his lips came not a sound. Marcia's head was bowed, but she had not closed her eyes, for she too was watching her father. She realized that he was unable to speak for the moment."May I say grace, Aunt Jo, just this once?" Jo winked an eye at her and nodded her approval. So with every head bowed, and every eye closed, except Maria's, Marcia said her first prayer. She wanted with all her heart to say: "And God bless Mama," but at that point she did hesitate and said "Aunt Jo" instead. As her "Amen" rang loud and clear, Sam begin waiting on Maria's plate. "What's wrong with you?" he asked. For it was obvious that his youngest daughter was pouting about something."You never let me say grace" she accused him. "You can say it next time." He promised. He attempted to reach for her hand, but he didn't. Sam served his own plate sparsely and passed the dishes containing the food on to Jo, who took for herself generous servings. Marcia, having overcome her desire to eat, had like Sam, taken very little on her plate

"Papa, when's Mama coming home?" Maria asked her father. Sam was unable to get his answer audible, so Jo answered for him. "Your Mama is not coming back." Marcia cried out:"Aunt Jo, don't tell her that; she's too little to understand." "Now you listen to me child." Jo said to Marcia. "We are never too little, or young, that is, to be told the truth. For we all know and God knows too, that your Mama will not be coming back." Sam half rose in an attempt to leave the table, but Jo took hold of his arm. "Sam, sit down. These children can never accept facts if you don't. Another fact is; they need you to help them, and you sure can't if you don't face things yourself." She hesitated then started again. "I know this doesn't seem likely the day to start, but no day will, until you do start. You must stand up Sam. Try hard not to fall short your duty to these girls." Sam did rise then and went droop-shouldered back to his and Eva's room. He stood looking out the end window thinking about what his sister had said. He knew Eva was gone forever. He didn't need Jo to tell him that. He had known since he picked his wife up from the ground in the garden, that she was gone.

It had been a rather warm day for the fall season, or maybe it was the piles of debris that he'd been burning in the lower pastures that was so warm. After the fires had burned out, he headed for the house, he recalled. It had been about lunch time anyway according to the sun's position.. After spending some thirty to forty minutes feeding the mules, he started toward the house .It was behind the barn in the pea patch that he had noticed something lying on the ground. He took a few long strides in that direction when he recognized Eva.

She had a new turnip patch coming up along side the peas, and there she lay in the middle of it with the cut turnips scattered all around her as well as all over her.

Sam stood staring down at her, shocked beyond reasoning and looking around for a clue of some explanation. He found none .He stooped over and gathered Eva into his arms and hurried on to the house. His guess was that she had merely fainted, though she was not pregnant to his knowledge .After laying her on the bed, he wet a rag and wiped her face. When she refused to awaken, startled he ran out of the house and went for Jo who lived down the road a short distance. He thanked Heaven that Jo was so near and hoped she would know what to do. While Jo had gone on to the house to stay with Eva, Sam put a saddle on his fastest nag and took off to get Doc Reeder Doc's old car was parked in front of his house, which meant Sam had found him in. He ran into Doc's office which was nothing more than half of his front porch walled up to make a room. Doc kept medicine there on his rough wooden shelves for most any ailment. Doc looked up startled as Sam came rushing through the only entrance to his cold unheated office. "It's Eva, Doc. She's fainted and I can't seem to bring her around. She's not pregnant." Sam picked up a stick outside Doc's gate on his way out, and after settling himself in the saddle, he gave the nag a thrashing across the buttocks. "Let's go, you damn raw bone, let's go". Doc and Jo were in the room with Eva when Sam got back. They heard him come in as he pushed the latch off the back door. They both met him outside Eva's door. Doc Reeder put his hand on Sam's shoulder. "I'm afraid there's nothing I can do Sam. Your wife is dead." "That's a lie." Sam shouted. "She just fainted Doc, she's not dead."

Sam attempted to enter Eva's room, but Jo grabbed his hand from the door knob. "Yes, she is dead Sam. Now come into the kitchen, I have some hot coffee brewing, and Doc wants to ask you something. And I want you to be agreeable." "Sam, I want permission,"Doc began," to examine Eva's body from head to heel. This will require taking all her clothes off however, which if necessary to examine as closely as I'd like for anything that might offer us a clue. Jo can assist me, if she would like, or if you would like." Jo was standing behind Sam's chair with both of her arms around him. "You must give permission, Sam," She insisted, Sam looked at Doc and merely nodded his head in approval. Jo and Doc returned to the back room. Sam jumped to his feet screaming after them." Wait Doc. How do you know she's dead? How can you make sure?" Again they carried him back to the kitchen.

Jo answered a faint knock on the back door and welcomed Mrs. Baggett. "I came as soon as Doc's wife told me. We're neighbors, you know." Noticing Sam who now had his upper body sprawled across the table, and Jo, who at the moment, had not ceased to cry. Mrs. Baggett turned to Doc. "Is there anything that I can do?" Doc hesitated a moment and then said, "Yes, come with me. Jo joined her brother in his grief while Mrs. Baggett assisted Doc. The thirty minutes they waited, seemed to be hours. As Doc re-entered the kitchen, Sam made no attempt to lift his head. Jo turned to Doc."Did you find anything?" Doc hesitated a moment observing Sam. "Yes." He replied. Doc sit down while Mrs. Baggett poured him a cup of strong coffee. "Sam." Doc gently called. Sam lifted his head and looked toward Doc with eyes that were too full to see him. "Your wife was bitten by a rattle snake. Since this area is working alive with them, I'm sure it was a rattler." "Where?" Sam managed to inquire. "Right between the breast. There are signs that she was bitten twice by the snake. She might have, at that point, had a heart attack." Sam again, let his head fall heavy across his folded arms.

Pastor George came and talked with Sam. "Sam. we need to plan the funeral arrangements." Sam snapped back,"There is not going to be one." The pastor mused for a moment, then responded. "Sam, we have to have a funeral. As sad as it is, it brings a closure for the family. It's the best way to let go. Your family and friends will be expecting a funeral." The pastor bowed his head. Sam bowed his head. Silence engulfed the room for a while. Finally, Sam lifted his head and spoke softly. "There will be no funeral. I don't want to go through that. Just burry Eva, and be done with it. Me and the girls cannot be involved in that. So. We will not talk about this again. Understand?" Pastor George gently rose to his feet, patted Sam on the shoulder, rubbed his hands across Sam's head, and quietly left the room.

Pastor George spoke with Jo on his way out. Jo was in a rage over Sam's decision, but she knew not to approach him. He was too crushed and angry. Jo knew she didn't need a fight today. Jo asked the pastor to oversee the arrangements. Pastor George made all the decisions with the funeral home based on Sam's wishes.

Sam was not aware of the knock on the door as the community women began dropping by bringing food for the family, and gifts for the children. Marcia came home from school and Maria had been awakened from her nap. Jo took both the girls out under the pecan trees to tell them about their Mama. Sam had found them there and took both of his weeping daughters into his arms. He had then walked out to the garden and looked the area over well. Jo and the girls followed him and helped in the search. They found nothing. Jo carried Maria on her back to the house. Sam walked with his arms around his oldest daughter who was now ten years old. He was concerned about his six year old, and he thanked God for Jo. Once he entered the house, he went straight to his room and closed the door behind him.

Suddenly, Sam turned from the window and came out of the room to re-join his family in the kitchen. He found Jo talking very motherly to his daughters. He stood quietly for a moment as he listened to Jo taking to the girls. "God gives and God takes."Jo was explaining." We don't know why, but we don't try to figure it out ourselves. We just know God has a plan. We also know the Lord loves us and will furnish our needs. You may not think so now, but you just wait and see for yourself. Anyway, heaven would be a lonely place if God never called an angel up there, and we know your Mama will glorify heaven. She will never feel another pain and God will make her happy forever. It's us who are here on earth that does all the suffering, not them that's in heaven. You know something else; your Mama won't ever again have to go out in the cold again to milk a kicking old cow. Isn't that wonderful?" Maria giggled. "Now you'll have to do it." She teased. Marcia smiled. "I love you very much, Aunt Jo,"she said warmly, putting her arm about her aunt's shoulder. Sam cleared his throat, and Jo saw him standing tall and straight in front of her. He too was smiling. Jo thanked God.

"Well, let's get up from the table, can't sit here all day. Marcia you clean up the dishes and Maria you dry them and put them away." Maria glared at Jo and said "I don't dry dishes." "Oh, yes you do." Jo answered. "Sam, you come with me. I'll check the laundry needs, in case a couple of dresses must be ironed for school tomorrow." Now it was Marcia who stared at Jo. "I'm not going to school anymore. I'm going to stay home and cook for Peps and take care of Maria." Jo smiled at her." Like fun you will. You will keep on doing the things you have always done, and going to school every morning is one of them. So let's not have any trouble about that." Jo shook her finger teasingly.

"Come on Sam." She tugged at his sleeve, and led him into the front bedroom, which was also used as a living room. Sam's house only had three rooms and two porches. In the summer months the porches were used as living rooms, and during the winter a fire was kept in the big fire place that faced both bed rooms. A couple of leather bottomed chairs were kept near both fireplaces. Long before the oak logs burned out at night, it was time to go to bed. A farmer never had time to sit around the living room. When his work was done and his supper eaten, he naturally removed his shoes and made ready for a good nights sleep. "Sit down Sam," Jo ordered him naturally. "I've got things all figured out." Sam smiled, "I'm glad Jo. Tell me what does a man do in my fix? If I had two little boys instead of girls, it would be easier. I could at least take them to the fields with me. I could teach them to plow, cut briars, sow seed, and manage to keep an eye on them." "Nonsense," Jo snapped."If you had boys I wouldn't know what to do myself. I never sewed a shirt in my life and don't know a thing about making all those pockets and placket things. It's girls that I know about. So you just sit there and listen without a word until I finish. And then be careful what you say." Sam couldn't help but be a little amused at his old maid sister. She would be a good back-bone for him, he knew that. He knew that he could always depend on Jo for any help his household needed. She had always been free with her sound advice, but unlike today, she usually waited until he asked for it. He understood Jo, and knew his choice now was to hear her out. She reminded him so much of their own mother who had been such a woman as Jo: strong, taking life in stride, crossing bridges as she approached them, and never failing to get across. He half smiled at this thought. Jo had the same blue eyes that their mother had, which never did go well with their temperament. They should have at least had brown eyes if not black, he thought. Jo could be a devil at times he knew, but she would also be an angel, and only then did her blue eyes compliment her. He smiled. Jo lived in a house exactly like his .In fact; it was the very house the two of them had been born in. Sam had used it as a pattern to build his own. The two of them owned a hundred acre farm together: it was given to them by their parents. Jo had helped Eva raise chickens, fatten pigs, and take care of the children. Eva had never been too healthy: she had a bad heart, and had always depended a little too much on Jo. Jo noticed Sam staring into the flames flickering up the back of the chimney. She also noticed the thin sheets of

13

suit clinging to the sides of the fireplace, and decided there had been much flickering of flames since there had been any swishing with a broom. But that could wait. She touched Sam's sleeve," Are you with me?" she whispered. "Yes, Jo."

"Well, it's like this," she began, "Like I told Marcia a minute ago, you must keep doing all the things you ever did, and keep going Sam. After all, Eva never did go to the fields and work with you. You did that alone. You've done all the farming and tended the live stock by your self. So it can't be any different now. Eva's passing only leaves her duties unattended, and you never did housework anyway, so that won't hinder you a bit, because there's where I come in. I can run the house and take care of the children, and with them, we can tend the chickens, and I will milk ole jersey every morning. That cow better know better than to kick me more than one time." Sam smiled and knew that the old devil was boiling up within her, but said nothing as his sister continued. "No need trying to iron out wrinkles unless I was ironing. It's time now to bed down for the night. I'm staying here Sam, and will sleep right there on the bed with the girls." Sam looked at her, "No that will make it too crowded for you. Maria can sleep with me." Jo snapped, "No, she can't either Sam. No need to start that. The child can't always be your bed-fellow. So just back your ears, grit your teeth, and go to bed. Heaven knows you sure look like you need some rest." Sam felt it too. In fact he was too weary and fatigue to argue the point and went on to his room, closing the door behind him. Jo busied herself for a short time, laying out the school clothes for the next day. Then, she and the girls too went to bed. They all needed rest, and needed it far more than they knew. Marcia and Maria were soon asleep, but sleep did not come quickly to Jo and Sam, who had too many things to figure out.

The routine of the following days were much like they had been. Sam went to the fields, the girls went to school, and Jo did the usual chores around the house. There never had been many chores done around the Marshall abode. Eva had never been a housekeeper; she did too much ailing and complaining to do anything that didn't have to be done. Let it go, was her philosophy. She did the things that had to be done, but nothing more. Eva never taught the girls to do anything. When they were not at school, they just played around the house and yards, instead of helping to keep the place orderly. Jo planned to correct that mistake. "Go fetch me a rake prissy pants." Jo said to Maria who was stepping as softly as a cat around the rose bush to catch a butterfly. "You go get it. "I'm busy." Maria did not even cast a glance at her aunt. Jo propped herself on the hoe handle with one hand thrust heavily on her hip." Listen to me child. There's going to be some changes made around here, and you're one of them." Maria glared at Jo. "What do you mean?" Jo glared back at her." You're going to show some respect for the rest of us, and the first one will be me. Why in no time at all, I'll be snapping my finger and you'll be marching. Like right now, you're going to march behind the house and bring me the rake." Maria thought about it for a moment, and then asked "And what if I don't?" Jo laid the hoe down on the ground and reached up over her head toward a dogwood tree. "I'll break myself a good switch while you think about it. If you think too long, I'll be using it on your behind." Maria forgot about the butterflies and headed toward the back yard. She had been gone much too long before she came back slowly dragging the rake behind her. She walked past where Jo stood, and let the rake fall to the ground, and kept walking to the road that ran in front of the house. There she half turned and gave her aunt a leer of indocility, then sit down picking up sand and sifting it through her fingers. Jo had stopped to lift the rake, but saw the leer plainly enough. Jo thought that one has got spunk, and plenty of it. Jo continued her task in solitude until most of the falling leaves had been raked together in one pile.

The Yuletide season was approaching and many preparations were to be made. She looked around at the leaves and other debris collected by October winds, and wished Sam would have fenced in the front yard as he had the back. Her efforts then would not be so futile. Come spring, she decided, there are going to be some flowers planted, but time enough for that. "First things first." She muttered to herself, gathering up the rake and gall-berry broom. Before departing to the rear of the house, she paused staring into the road at the pouting child. "It's not her fault," she deliberated. The child has never been taught to be useful. Having no chores of her own, she never learned anything about responsibility. These grounds would be an excellent place to start. "Maria, go fetch the wheel barrow and pile these leaves into it." "The wheelbarrow is too heavy for me." she answered Jo, speaking each word as though she was actually spelling it. "You are not a baby anymore. You are a big girl, and pushing an empty wheelbarrow won't hurt you. I'll roll it to the back myself, after you get it filled. And we'll have a big camp fire back there tonight. It's too dangerous to start a fire here in front, with no fence to help to keep control over it." Jo had more than half the back yard raked, wondering if Maria would obey her this time, and allowing her plenty of time to do so before she checked. A sneak view around the corner of the house revealed the barrow piled high and over-flowing with leaves, and Maria again setting in the road sifting sand. Jo returned the barrow after disposing of its load, and called out pleadingly, "Fill it again dear, and let me know this time when you're finished." Maria sprang to her feet and hurriedly approached her task, tossing leaves by the armload into the barrow. She then dashed spiritually to the back where Jo was sweeping. She yelled brusquely." Ready!" Her indignation went un-noticed by Jo who was searching in thought for the proper means of discipline. A good spanking would be in order no doubt, but this child had never really had one. Jo didn't have too much faith in sparing the rod, but this one would probably go into a spell of tantrums if she laid one hand upon her. No, she decided, there just had to be another way.

Love and kindness, she knew, were often sufficient tools to work with, if one only had the patience to use them. She lifted her head upward looking toward the low hanging white clouds that were sailing slowly above her. Then she gazed above them into the blue, wondering how much time it really took for a child to readjust after having its foundation pulled from beneath it. She whispered, "Look down on us dear Lord, please guides us in the direction we should go." She was still standing in her daze when Marcia came out to greet her. "Have you had a good day, Aunt Jo?" Jo came out of her trance and answered her. "Very good, and how was school?" "School was fine, and I am hungry. Is there something I can eat now? And do you want me to do anything? You look tired." Marcia then turned to go into the house. She stopped short, looking around observing the grounds. "This place has never looked so good. You must have worked all day. Where is Maria?" Jo smiled. "Go on in and put your books up. Supper is already cooked and still hot. Butter yourself a biscuit now, and I'll be in later. Maria is out front." Marcia kissed her aunt on the cheek." I love you," she said, then took off for a biscuit sandwich. Jo wondered how two girls brought up by the same parents could be so different, yet so much alike. Since neither of them had been taught responsibility, their indolence was indeed legitimate. So far, they had lived in and accepted the environment of a sty. A child seldom is expected to uplift himself above that of the other inhabitants about him. Jo had always frowned upon the untidy conditions kept at her brother's house, but until now however, she'd had no opportunity and certainly no right to attempt changing things. Having kept her place so immaculate for so many years made her sick to her stomach to tolerate anything less. She had, in the past, strived to keep her nose where it belonged, and now that it belonged here, her intentions were to waste no time in putting a polish on this place. With God given strength, she'd have things orderly and controllable 'fore the Yuletide. She anticipated no obstacles in her endeavors once she opened their eyes to the fruits of labor.

Jo had found much pleasure in her inner desire to work. She had found too, that the devil plays with idle hands. This recollection brought her mind back to Maria and to the fact too that she had finished her work, and was just standing like a statue in the yard. Jo went into the house to see what, if indeed anything was going on. Marcia, sitting at the dinning table munching on her biscuit and leafing through a book, looked up as Jo entered the room. "What are you going to do now?" she inquired. "Rest," Jo whispered, taking herself a seat at the table. Marcia closed her book and sit staring. "What's on your mind?" Jo wanted to know. "O, nothing. I was just looking out the widow." Jo thought for a moment, then stated," Looking at it maybe, but not out it, with all the grease and grime it's caked with." Marcia shifted her stare at Jo. She had detected an air of indifference in her tone. Jo was weary and had been a bit snappy, she realized. "There's some tea cakes in that pan." she pointed to a white pan sitting on the cook table. "Been cooking, raking, and baking all day. You go out and fetch your sister in, and I'll pour us some milk. When you get back, we'll just sit here and have little party, and talk about things." Jo had the milk poured and a plate of tea cakes placed on the oil-clothed table before the girls came in. She sits down again wishing she knew a way to break down and destroy that little wall Maria had built around herself. Then, with no precognition of Maria's thoughts, she was awed as the child approached her with an arm full of goldenrods that she'd been gathering when Marcia found her. Without a word of comment, Maria placed the flowers in Jo's lap. "O, my goodness." Jo exclaimed. "Are these for me?" Jo asked. "Of course they are." Maria answered her with a manner of causality. She then took a few steps backwards to escape the reach of her aunt's out-stretched arms. Jo had intended to give her an affectionate pat on the arm, but due to the circumstances, she instead arose from her chair. Trying to hide her mutilated feelings, she whispered: "Thank you very much. Goldenrods are so pretty. I'll put them in a jar of water right now. Thank you." Maria sneered, "there's just weeds." After Jo had cut off the stems to fit the flowers into a jar, she returned to the table where the girls were still sipping their milk. She carefully placed the arrangement in the center of the table. She reclaimed her own place at the table, smiled and said, "Yes, they are only weeds, but look at them now. So simple, yet so beautiful, It's like bringing sunshine into a dark room. Don't you think?" The girls looked at each other then at Jo who was still glowing. Letting their eyes feast on the goldenrods, they both burst into laughter. And so did Jo. She had never in her life seen so much beauty in a goldenrod, nor had they ever before offered her such a great sense of achievement. Now with a real party atmosphere, Jo thought this would be the appropriate time to begin teaching a lesson. "It's a funny thing," she began, "How little things can play such a big roll, and how simple things can become so great. Notice how a vase of flowers can bring warmth to a cold room, how it can fill a room with happiness and bring light to its darkest corners. It's the same with most simple things. A chirping bird can lift a heavy heart, a needle and thread can make a lovely gown, mansions are built with hammer and nails. And with only a handful of seed, gardens can grow. All these simple things must be put into the hands of people who will use them." she concluded. "Soap and water can make us clean, and it can clean our clothes." Maria added." That's right," Jo agreed, "And when soap and water is put to good use, it can clean our floors and windows." She added. Marcia noticed again the window panes and agreed. "I wish our house looked like yours Aunt Jo." After a brief pause, Jo added, "It can. And I will help you girls all I can, but I will not do it alone. I'll make each of us a list and then we'll get started. While you girls clean the windows, I'll sew some curtains." Jo promised.

The projects got under way, and in the weeks that followed there was much team work and unity in the Marshall home. Jo mixed some concoction with lime water, and with a sage broom, she white washed the interior of the three rooms. Then with a shuck scrub and lye water, she had the wooden floors clean enough to eat from. From Lundy's grocery she purchased a can of enamel and gave the girls a lesson in painting. The three iron beds and leather bottomed chairs took on a look of brilliancy. Finishing the window curtains with a fancy strip of rickrack, Jo adorned the widows. From her own house, she brought two sheepskins, placing them along side the beds. With an elated ego, she greatly admired her accomplishments. She indeed did much more than she allowed herself credit for. Marcia and Maria had both been very helpful. Though Maria had shown little enthusiasm, it was obvious to Jo that both girls were well pleased with the results of their efforts. It appeared to her too, that Maria was really more concerned than Marcia. Even though Marcia had done her chores willingly enough, she had no foresight to speak of, and Jo had to point each thing out to her. While Maria was capable of keeping herself busy, she did it more reluctantly than willing. Jo wondered if she really did resent the work, or if she merely wanted her to think so. It was not an easy task trying to coop with and comprehend Maria's moods and endeavors. One thing Jo was sure grateful for, she had no trouble reading Marcia, she concluded. Marcia was after all the most agreeable of the two. She did what she was told to do, but seldom anything more. Actually she was not so indolent, as dense Jo decided.

Marcia had been doing most of the cooking while project clean up had been in operation. So, as far as Jo was concerned, that fact alone was equivalent enough to eradicate her short comings in the project itself. No, she was not at all worried about Marcia, who would not speak sharply at a mongrel, or swat a fly. It was Maria that stole most of her contemplations. Jo herself being somewhat illiterate as well as verdant was really not capable of analyzing personal behavior to any intelligent concepts. She was not too naïve however, to form valuable opinions. And she was brave enough to act on intuitions. Adverse to intimate conversations, she had fled on all occasions in which such had occurred. She knew it was time now to have a talk with Marcia about the birds and bees, but she could never bring herself to the hideous environment of such intimacy. Anyway, if the girl would just keep her eyes open, she'd learn enough. That was the only learning she had had. Jo was by no means satisfied with her conclusion, and knew it was not right to let a young lady grow up ignorant to the facts of life. Though a certain amount of innocence was expected of the nice ones, God, himself had given us enough brains for common sense, only if we would use it. That would usually be enough to help ourselves out of hot water. Ratifying herself for having at least common sense and assuring herself that Marcia had as much, she let the whole train of thought escape her for the time being.

As Jo entered the Marshall home the next morning, she brought with her an arm load of holly branches, bearing an abundance of red berries. As Marcia answered her aunt's rap on the door, she found her patting her foot and humming Jingle Bells. Jo skipped across the threshold with a hearty "Ho, Ho, Ho." After unburdening herself from the holly branches, she sang out, "Deck the Halls With Holly," She grabbed Marcia by both hands dancing around singing "Dashing Through The Snow." Marcia danced around as though she had wooden legs. Jo let go of her and reached to Maria, who was so light one her feet and vivacious enough to add a few steps of her own. Both girls joined Jo in singing the carols. Not only was Jo breathless when the dancing ceased, she was also amazed that it had ended in the kitchen. "How did we get in here?" she asked Maria. "We just danced right in." Maria giggled. Jo placed an arm around each girl." Since we are already in the kitchen, Marcia you make cocoa. Maria, you come with me and we'll decorate the kitchen with red berries too." Jo kept singing. "O.K. Jo, lets go," Maria sang out. The kitchen was filled with laughter as each person turned about to do her chores. While arranging the holly branches across the mantel, Jo quietly thanked God for helping her to mold a good mood for this day. She did not feel up to all this gala herself, especially the dancing, since her rheumatism had been flaring up. She whispered to God about that condition too, but she did not remain quiet too long. She dared not to now, lest she set an atmosphere o f melancholy. "God, forbid." She said aloud. Maria didn't hear her, for she was still Dashing Through the Snow. Jo retreated to find Marcia filling the cups to their capacity with steaming cocoa. In fact, had overfilled one, Jo observed, as she blotted up the small pool from the table. They took their cups into the front room and sit by the fire, where they sipped luxuriously on the drinks. "Aunt Jo, tell of some ghost stories." Marcia pleaded. "Ghost stories?" Jo exclaimed, a bit startled. "It's no time to be telling stories like that; it's time for stories about the Christ child. You know that as well as I do. Let's all sing The Star of Bethlehem." Again Jo led in the singing, and the girls joined in. Jo noticed that Marcia was not really singing with them, except for a word now and then. She was, instead, staring at the holly on the mantel. Something was gnawing at her, Jo knew, but then try with all her might, she could not keep all the sadness out of Christmas. Singing the carols tended to change the spirit from that of laughing and dancing. Jo was trying to think of something to say or do that would bring Marcia back to them. Marcia interrupted the singing. "Let's go to the cemetery." "What for?" asked Maria. "To visit your mother's grave." Jo told her.

Noticing the tears dripping down Marcia's cheeks, Jo dropped her own head reverently. "God, help me again." She uttered. "Well, let's see." Jo began. "We are about ready for ole St. Nick except for the tree. We can chop one down while we're strolling around a bit. Get your sweaters." Maria announced "I'm not going." Jo looked at her "Yes you are." This would be their first visit to the cemetery. Jo had thought about it herself, but has decided to wait until after the holidays were over. She wished now that Marcia had waited until then to mention it. Jo got the hatchet from the back porch and the three of them sojourned. It was no more than a mile down the path to the cemetery. Jo thought how nice it would be, should it be ten miles, or at least a distant too far to walk. But it was not! Visiting a cemetery certainly had never been a journey that pleased her. She believed in letting the dead rest undisturbed. "What's gone is gone" was her outlook. She had never mourned too long for something that was gone. She had feelings, same as everyone else, but had sense enough to know what 'gone' meant. One should not cry over spilled milk. The church setting beneath tall pines never looked more deserted, nor as cold, as it did this day. A heavy layer of straw covered the ground like a brown carpet. Amid trees so tall and grounds so massive, the church itself looked hardly larger than a shoebox. Jo deliberately shifted her glance toward the burial grounds that appeared even more eerie. They found the gate open, which was most unusual, unless of course, there were others in the vicinity. Uneasily, Jo leered in all directions, but didn't see another living soul. Her squeamish feelings were very unusual too, and she wished she could make conversation; if only she could stop thinking so daffy. Letting her eyes now rest on Eva's grave, she suddenly stood still, and reached to grasp a hand on either side of her. Astonished, she looked first at Marcia, then at Maria. They too stood in bewilderment. A wide area around Eva's grave had been swept clean. On top of the grave was a garland of holly. "Sam did it," Jo decided. She and Marcia stood for a time in mediation as Maria left them to read epitaphs from the scarcely scattered tombs. Marcia began sobbing again, and Jo held her close to her until Maria reunited with them. "Let's go now." Jo suggested. "Let's go into the church." Maria pleaded "No!" Jo told her. "Please, let's do." Marcia pleaded. Agreeing without desire, Jo led the way to the chapel. She asked the girls to wait and let her see if the door was locked. She turned the knob gently and cautiously pushed the door open. With one eye, she peered through the narrow opening of the door. The sanctuary was dark except for a lone candle flickering near the alter. Jo blinked her eyes in an effort to clear her apparently blurred vision. Was it a man she saw kneeling there, or was it shadows created by the flickering candle fooling her? She blinked her eyes again. Truly it was no apparition she saw. It was Sam Marshall. Recognizing him, Jo guided her steps softly backward, easing away from the door. Marcia and Maria were watching her, knowing that she had spied something or someone. Jo was shaking and very pale as she pulled a rag from her apron pocket and dabbled her eyes. Her voice quivered as she whispered," We can't go in there." Maria, with both hands over her mouth, asked" Why?' Jo was quiet for a moment. "Because someone is in there." She managed to reply, and directed her trio homeward.

Jo was unaware of the wind and cold as they walked along the same route home again. She wished, for once, she had not given in to Marcia's whims. Yet, it seemed to her the compassionate thing to do. She understood too, the girl's desire to visit her mother's grave. If only the visit could have been at another time. Any other time, she thought, would no doubt been more appeasing, at least for her. She had not revealed who she saw, and the girls did not ask. She wondered if either, or indeed both of them, suspected the truth; but if they did, they displayed no evidence. Being dismayed herself, Jo offered no comfort to Marcia who quietly sobbed behind her nor to the complaints of Maria who ran ahead kicking up leaves, as she searched for lost coins. Maybe she had neglected Sam more than she should have lately, but there had been so much to do getting ready for the holidays, that were already too near, she'd not given much time to him. But goodness sake, she thought, wasn't it enough trying to keep his daughters happy. She suspected however, what

Sam needed most, she could not give him. A man needed more than clean linens on his bed. She had sympathy for him, but there was a limit to what a sister could do. In her condolence, tears blurred her vision; she wiped her eyes, and said to herself, "Like I always say, crying is no cure for anything. A man has to stand tall and strong, lest he become too weak to support those who lean upon him. And everybody is needed for support to someone. Sam should be here right now to offer a little support for his oldest daughter, and to speak a word about behavior to the youngest. The way Sam has been acting lately, he's no support to himself. Sam never comes home before dark anymore, then eats and goes straight to bed. He could talk to them sometimes, and if he doesn't soon smile, his face will crack when he does". Marcia, wiping her face, stepped up beside Jo. "I'm sorry." she said." But I don't cry too much anymore .I'm worried about Peps too. Don't be too hard on him Aunt Jo .He's so lonely for her." Maria came back to meet them." What did you say?" she asked Jo."I said stop your foolishness and look for a Christmas tree." Marcia looked at Jo."Oh, Aunt Jo, do we have to get it today?" "Yes." Jo retorted. "Christmas is coming just as always, and it will not wait for you nor Paps to get the spirit. Here, you take this hatchet and follow Maria."

So, through the woods they did indeed follow Maria who again ran ahead, as lively as a filly. "Let's get one as tall as the ceiling." She suggested. "And who will decorate it?" Jo asked. "Alright," Maria agreed." We'll get a short one, and I'll decorate it myself." Jo pondered."You will do no such thing. Everybody will take a part in decorating the tree. So, you will have some help." "Let her do it Aunt

Jo. She's so young, and she wants to do it." Jo embraced Marcia." Listen to me child; she is lots bigger than you think. Age has nothing to do with it. Maria is not as innocent as you think she is. You must help with the tree; you'll feel much better once we start tossing the pretties upon it. Anyway, you stop concerning yourself so much about Maria, and think about yourself some. You need to honey." Marcia smiled, and Jo's spirits were elated. Jo wanted a pine, but one of good size and shape was too difficult to find. Marcia suggested a cedar, which grew plentiful about them and which she thought would make a more appropriate tree for the occasion. The woods were filled with cedar, and it was easy to make a decision among them. Marcia chopped away with the hatchet, then gave it to Jo to finish cutting the tree down. Jo looked around for Maria and found her swinging from a pine top. Marcia spied a squirrel playing friskily around a Black Gum tree, and called her sister to come see. Maria then attempted to catch the creature for herself a pet, persuading Marcia to assist her. Things were looking merrier to Jo, who couldn't force herself to stop thinking about Sam. The girls were now less sorrowful. Funny about those two, she thought, one displaying her true emotions, while the other one strived to hide as much. Maria, she knew was not apathetical, and her ability to appear blithe was not to be scoffed, as fallacious as it was. The tree fell to the ground with a light thud that brought the girls back to where Jo stood beside it." How will you get it home?" Maria inquired. "I won't," Jo stated. "You two will each grab a limb and drag it." "All the way home?" the youngest inquired again. "All the way home." Jo insisted. "Unless you want to decorate it right here. It's your tree." The two sisters each took hold a brace and headed back to their road, sweeping a path in which Jo followed. "Dashing Through The Snow." Maria began to sing. Marcia made no attempt to join in and help her.

The woods were filled with the rustle of the season. The leaves fluttered and drifted from one place to another, before finally settling upon the thick layer on the ground. A forest of pines formed a green background for the magnificent colors still lingering in the woods. Jo took a deep breath filling her lungs with the cool and refreshing air. Looking about her at the abstracts painted by nature was very stimulating. Almost all the trees had shed their leaves, but all had not. The pines and the cedars could be relied upon to forever cover the wood lands with a shelter of green. The red leaves of the Dogwood and Persimmon glowed beautifully against the setting sun, while the Poplar and Birch offered their brilliant hues of yellow. Looking upward, she observed the smoky-blue horizon, revealing a spectrum of color. The low drifting clouds waltzed lazily above her. "Going to be a heavy frost in the morning." she said to herself. "Who are you talking to, Aunt Jo?" Maria was looking back at her. "Talking to myself." Jo told her, still searching the horizon. "I said it's fixing to snow." Maria laughed." I wish it would. Do you really think so?" Jo questioned Maria," Well, what do you think?" Maria pondered a moment "I don't think it will snow, because it never has-not in my lifetime." "That makes good sense." Jo assured her. The beauty and the mystery of the woods offered so much contentment that Jo hated to have her vista disturbed by returning to the house. Perhaps there, she thought, serenity could be achieved if the girls would only apply themselves to the adornment of the tree. She had already brought some trinkets from her own house. The girls were already having a little squabble, but nothing serious, Jo observed. Maria would walk too fast, then suddenly stop, creating difficulty in their team-work. Marcia kept protesting, and Maria, of course, kept denying it all.

Finally home again; the tree was left at the back door until a stand could be built for it. Jo asked Maria to go find a piece of wood around the barn, or the corn crib. She then told Marcia to fetch some nails from the kitchen. So, together, a cross was nailed to the bottom of the cedar, and Jo took it indoors. "Now, where shall we stand it?' Jo asked. "On the dinning table." Maria suggested. "That's crazy." Marcia informed her." Let's see." sighed Jo, looking about the front room, which was plenty large enough to accommodate the cedar. The room had scarcely any furnishings in it. Jo had hung curtains over the three windows, and did not want to hide them with the tree. She stood with her back to the fireplace, which was situated in the middle of one wall. With the front entrance door to her left, and the door leading into the back room to her right, her decision was not easy. Across the room were two beds, and against the wall between them was a night stand. At the foot of one bed was a trunk. "Oh, we have plenty of room!" she exclaimed. "First, let's to some re-arranging. Let's put the tree in a corner. This devilish room, as big as it is, don't have but two corners because of a dadburn door in the other two." The girls laughed. They liked to see Jo get out-done; she seemed to make such a fuss about it. Jo pushed the old trunk over by the window."Grab hold of this bed and let's push it over to that corner." Maria complained, "I like my bed between the windows." Jo smiled." Well right now, we will put it in the corner where beds belong. Then we'll put the tree in the other corner. Then, all the curtains will show and the windows will allow light to shine through on the tree."

Jo was silently wishing for a living room "There's still enough stone and rock lying around this place to build a mansion, if one was mind to work a little for it."I'll talk to Sam about adding one big room across the front of this house, before we put up another Christmas tree. I'll bring my old organ down here, and the couch, then you girls can have a living room." Marcia was getting very excited over that idea, "Aunt Jo, I hope Paps will do it." Jo smiled. "I hope so too, but if he wont, I can get somebody else to build it. Most of the men are kind of idle this time of the year. And we make enough extra money off the peanuts to pay for the labor." Both girls, wide-eyed, rushed over to Jo and embraced her. Jo placed an arm around both of them and began swirling them around." Dancing around the Christmas tree, the Christmas tree, the Christmas tree." She sang. And to her jollity the girls joined in and sang with her. "You know what; I'm going to bring my organ down here tomorrow, somehow or other." She promised. "I can't play anything by the books, but I can do well enough by ear.

So, tomorrow night we will be singing by music." Maria jumped up and down with glee. "Could you teach me to play, Aunt Jo?" Jo wished she could. "No child, I can't read a note myself, but you can learn like I did, by just playing around with it. Now you two start tossing glitter upon the tree, and I'll step outside and make mental plans for our living room. "What's going on?' a masculine voice asked. Startled, they all jumped at Sam standing in the doorway.

"Plenty is going on Sam. Step outside with me, and I'll tell you part of it now." Jo opened the door, and Sam followed her. The sisters finished decorating the tree with gaiety. It was not their first tree, but it was, without a doubt, their largest and most picturesque. Stepping back to the fireplace, they admired their artistic talents. "Do you think we'll have a surprise?" Maria wondered. "Yes, there will be at least one. There always has been. Aunt Jo is sewing something." Marcia confided in her sister. "I want something besides clothes and a doll. I'm really too big for dolls anyway. I want a record player." Maria whispered. Marcia then expressed her own desire for a radio. "The Readers has one and I heard them say that they could hear people singing in Nashville." She had wondered about this, but never questioned it. Maria, not being very observant of grown-up conversations, admitted she had never heard of it. "I think we'll get a new dress and a coat." Marcia stated. She had legitimate reasons for guessing the truth, for she had already seen the red and green corduroy that Jo had purchased. What she had not seen, was the yards of fabric that still lay on Jo's machine, and the paper bag sitting in her kitchen holding red vases. "Let's make some more cocoa for Paps and Aunt Jo," Marcia suggested. Maria, who wanted some for herself, agreed. They left the fireside as Jo and Sam re-entered the room. Observing the adorned room for the first time, Sam made mention of it. "Sure looks like Christmas, he said. "Done me good to walk in on all that dancing. The girls have already forgotten haven't they?" Jo did not comment. Forgot about what? She wondered. If he meant what she thought he did, her answer would have been a loud and clear "NO!" She avoided mentioning the afternoon events. She planned to talk with him about that, and about his own withdrawn behavior, but this was not the time to do so.

Jo had managed to obtain Sam's permission to have the additional room built. It could hardly be considered a task, since he willingly agreed to any suggestions she voiced. She had told him too, of the gifts planed for the girls and the food she planned to purchase and prepare. Sam had said he was grateful to her, but he seemed more numb to her that grateful. Finally Sam was able to speak more sincerely. "There's not much you can't do, is there Jo? Take that tree." he nodded toward the corner. "You chopped it down, got it home, and made a stand. Look at the walls how pretty and white; you managed that yourself. And you can build that room you want without any help from me. You are a very good person." Jo looked up at his pale and lean face. "Stop your nonsense Sam. There's plenty I wish I could do. You have done more for me Sam, than I could ever do for you, and you know what I mean." Sam was silent for only a moment."Been thinking about you having to come up here every morning, working all day, then going back home every night. It's getting too cold now for you to keep that up. I wish you could make some arrangements to come up here and stay. Course, I know you've got your own place, but we could let it out to share croppers." Jo stormed out," Share croppers? What in the tarnation would we do with them? This place is not a bit too big for us to handle. We've been doing it. Sam, are you sick or something? What ails you anyhow? Sam shook his head. "Just thought how much easier it would be for you and the girls to stay in the same place, since you are always here anyway, taking care of things. I've already spoken with Lou Ayers about it, and he is interested, since he has to make a move before the first of the year anyway. He lost his lease on that little patch he's been tending." Sam must be sick Jo thought. Not knowing what comments to make, Jo remained silent. She was glad when

Marcia called out that the cocoa was ready. Jo tugged at Sam's sleeve;" Let's go," Sam had no taste for cocoa tonight, and so stated, as he turned and went into his room closing the door behind him. Jo stood staring at the door until a light shown beneath it, and a sound of shuffling papers she heard. Marcia was tugging at her sleeve, so she joined the girls alone. Always something to spoil everything, she thought. "Marcia, you make a fine cup of cocoa." She commented. "I made it too." Maria proclaimed." Well, I'm proud of you." Jo answered. "Aunt Jo, can you teach me to sew and do some needle work?" Marcia wanted to know." I can and will teach you, both of you." Jo promised. "I don't want to learn." Maria snapped. "I want to pick a guitar and whistle." Jo looked at her and said "You'll have to learn on your own. "But first, you can clean up these cups and put them away. I'm not going home tonight. I'm too tired to walk. I'll sleep with you Maria. By the way, I've got some good news. We're going to have that room I mentioned. Then I'll put my bed in the room with yours, and just move in with you. How about that?" Marcia ran excitedly, kissed Jo on the cheek, and asked, "Are you really? I will be so happy if you do." Maria ran and jumped into Jo's lap. With both arms around her, she yelled," Me too." Jo cautioned her, "Not so loud, your Pap has already gone to bed." Jo stood up smiling triumphantly, "Goodness sake, if I had known it would've made you this happy. I'd have moved in years ago." The three laughed with glee.

Then, the laughter subsided abruptly at the sound of a shot. Jo immediately sat down."Oh, God .No!" she cried. Marcia made a dash for her father's door. Jo jumped up and stopped her. "Don't go in there." She begged. "Sit down, both of you. Let me go." Jo found Sam relaxed on his bed, with his head resting against his pillow. Blood was gushing from his temple. Jo fell to her knees by his bed, reaching his hand that she held clasped between her own, and sorrowfully she moaned." Why, why did you do this to me and the girls? God knows we've been through enough burdens lately. Why, Sam?" She lifted her head and looked at him questionable. But Sam Marshall uttered not a word. Jo left Sam's room and called Doc. She told him that Sam was dead. Doc got in touch with the funeral home, and headed toward the Marshalls. When Doc arrived he found both of the girls in Jo's arms. The three of them were weeping speechles .Doc put his arms around them. The four of them went into Sam's room.

The girls screamed as they looked at Sam staring up at them. "What is your plan?" Doc asked. Jo answered."A funeral tomorrow afternoon at the church. You get in touch with pastor George and work it out with him," Doc was silently surprised. Jo must really be down. He had never seen her so calm and quiet. Sure, Sam was her only brother, and no sister, but he couldn't imagine Jo being so quiet.

The knock on the door alerted Jo. She took the call. The pastor walked with her back to Sam's room He hugged the girls, and said a prayer for them. He told Jo that the men from the funeral home were outside. He suggested that they leave the room. Leaving that room was the hardest thing Jo could recall having to endure. She placed her arms around the girls and led them into the kitchen. Pastor George and Doc stayed in the room until Sam's body was taken out. Then they went into the kitchen and tried to calm the girls. Marcia cried out, "Now, me and Maria has nobody." Jo grabbed her, "O, yes you have. You both have me." Pastor George spoke up."I am always with you. You can count on me if there's ever anything I can do for you."

It was an awesome night .No one went to bed. Around midnight Doc left. Jo and the girls slept in their chairs, then on the floor. It was daybreak before all three of them got into the same bed.

Mrs. Baggett came early. She had made arrangements for food and drinks throughout the day.Doc came to drive the ladies to the funeral. All arrangements had been thoughtfully planed and accomplished with ease. The girls couldn't talk for crying. So they too were quiet. Doc sat with them at the funeral. He had an arm around Jo. The girls noticed-especially Maria. The flag-draped casket sat in front of them. They were in control until the Star Spangle Banner was played. Sam had been a soldier, and was so recognized. Jo sobbed with her head on Doc's shoulder. Doug came and sit by Marcia with one arm around her. Jo placed her arm around Maria. As the casket was removed from the chapel to the cemetery, Marcia screamed. Jo glanced at her and she was in Doug's arms. Maria cried out and Jo pulled her closer to her. Doc tightened his hold on Jo. As soon as the casket was out, Doc said to Jo, "Let's go and come back tomorrow to view the finished grave." They both stood up. Jo pulled Maria up, and motioned for Maria. Doug said, "I'll take Marcia home."

The ladies had the table set. It was full of food and variety. Iced tea was served, and pretty linen napkins were on the table. Marcia and Maria ate quiet well. But Jo was not hungry. Doc persuaded her to, at least, eat something. Pastor George prayed a blessing on the food and the family. Jo, looking around the room, came to her senses. With all this many friends, why worry? It also occurred to Jo that she was not in control. God was. As soon as the last guest left, Jo and the girls went to bed for a nap. That was Doc's suggestion. "You didn't sleep last night, and you are tired. A nap will be a great blessing. Sometimes, it's better than an aspirin."Jo kissed Doc on the cheeks and responded, "I will." And she did.

It was Christmas Eve and all was quiet except for the grand-father's clock which struck loud and enshrouded, keeping pace with time. Jo studied the old clock for a time wishing that she too, could forever move forward never to be concerned with the past; that each hour could be struck off and forgotten. She took a seat on her organ bench and began to play "Auld Lane Sine." Marcia ran to her," Stop it! You know we shouldn't have music." Maria asked."Why not?" "Yes." Jo whispered," Why not?" After a moment's hesitation, Jo walked over to the grand father clock and picked up a Bible from beside it. "Now, that's more like what we should be doing." Marcia said. Jo opened the Bible to the book of Samuel while both girls observed her. Jo began," It has been said that unhappiness can be charmed away with the sound of music. Here we find David with his harp, playing music for Saul, which refreshed him, made him well, and departed the evil spirits from him. I think one of the fairest and most glorious gifts of God is music. In Psalms we read of the music of the sanctuary, which says, Praise Him with the sound of trumpets, harp, and tumbrel. Praise Him with stringed instruments, organs, and the loud cymbals." Jo closed the book and reclaimed her position at the organ, where together the three of them sang Auld Lane Sine and Away in the Manger. Jo passed out the gifts, then with the Bible in her hands again, she read and prayed. "Lord have mercy upon us. Oh God, be clear when thou judge me. Hide thy face from our sins, and blot out our iniquities. Create within us clean heart, and renew a new spirit within us. Show us the way you want us to go. Let peace be within us."

In the months that followed, Jo was a true example of the characteristic qualities governed by Jupiter, the planet under which she was born. She had perhaps too many negotiations with Lou Ayers, for it was near planting time before he got settled into her house. The fields had been cleared, but the land had not been plowed. The guano and seed were stored in the barn loft waiting to be put into the ground. She feared the rains would get started before Lou did. With him, she planned their acreage, to the extreme of drawing him a map, showing him precisely the crops she intended to grow, as well as the exact spot on which she planned to grow them. Though Lou, at times, got somewhat irritated with her, he was also amused at her. From time to time, she would stroll to the particular areas in which he was supposed to be working for an eye witness of his activities. On such occasions, she often found his mule nibbling the grass at the end of the rows, the plow fallen over on its side, and Lou sitting in the shade of a tree. Standing at a distance, she would watch him until he finally pulled himself up and again took over management of the mule and plow. Agitated with contempt for his idleness, she would start back toward the house to check on the carpenters who too seemed to take too many breaks. Determined to get her crops planted and the house renovated before Easter was, to say the least, a great burden. But she would do it; she vowed again and again. It was not her nature to falter. She had little patients with people like Lou Ayers who appeared to be easily led, but had no initiative of their own. "I wonder what sign Lou was born under." She said to Marcia. "What sign were you born under?" Marcia asked. Well, I'm a Sagittarian." Jo boasted. "What is that?" Marcia wanted to know. Jo thought for a moment than began: "It's what I am. A Sagittarian can do twice the work that many others can, and we are happier people too. The Bowman is one of our signs, and that means we are always aiming at something. When we set our heads to do something, we do it. Some of us kill our fool selves though with over zeal." Marcia asked,"What is zeal?" Jo smiled at her and then replied: "Don't worry about it honey, you don't have any."

Jo was reminded now of the talk she had been planning to have with Marcia about her grades. "Your grades don't please me. Isn't it about time you started to get serious about your school work? Are you pleased with your grades? Don't you realize that you are the one in charge of them? You are the only one who can pull them up and only then if you really want to. So, what are you going to do, pass or fail?" Marcia was quiet for a while, then mumbled," I don't know." Jo was concerned. Marcia was always dragging her feet when she walked, and whining when she talked. She was slow. Jo looked at her," I'm going to start you on some chill tonic." Marcia replied quickly," Aunt Jo, I have never had a chill." Jo explained.

"It's the iron in the tonic that you need." Though Marcia was failing in her grades, the bad marks never seemed to bother her. Mrs. Baggett had called on Jo to discuss the matter. "It's a very serious situation." She began. "You see, this is a repeat of the grade she failed last year. To fail it again indicates a lack of desire and determination or either an immature mentality. What do you think Miss Marshall?" Jo realized now, she was starring at the teacher. She was embarrassed, and shifted her position, placed her hands on her hip, pulled her limp frame erect and answered." yes." Mrs. Baggett smiled at Jo and asked again." What do you think Miss. Marshall?" Jo snapped. "I'll have to give the matter some thought."

Now, Jo had given as much thought to Marcia's grades as she had time for. With her seed in the ground, and the house finished, she would search for Marcia's mental block. There was a time when she thought Marcia was going to be a smart person, then behold, she turned lazy over night. Jo knew the girl had gone through enough to take the wind out of her sail, but it was time to get on a new path. "Aunt   Jo, may I go to bed?" Marcia asked. Jo saw that she was upset and excused her. Jo got Maria to aid her in searching for her Zodiak book. She had never looked up Marcia's sign, but now she felt the need to do so. Until she had done so, she knew she could not understand her. Maria found the book in the organ bench and handed it to Jo. "What's the book about Jody?" "You little imp." Jo laughed." It's about people. It tells what they are like and what   they're made of." "What am I made of?" Maria wanted to know. Jo smiled again," Same thing I am. We were both born under the same sign. Now off to bed and leave me to ponder." Jo lit a lamp and pulled a chair close to the library table, turning the pages in her book until she found the birth date of Marcia. Her sign was Cancer, the crab. Reading now, Jo made short mental notes of those born under this sign. Their moods and temperaments often became as changeable as their governing planet, the moon. They were inclined to cling to tradition and live in the past, very sensitive but seldom show it. Criticism hurts them, and crab-like, they crawl into their shells .Even changes in the weather affect their restless nature. These people are home loving, fond of family, affectionate, sympathetic, and loyal. Yet, due to the lack of emotional display, they are often misunderstood and unappreciated. Glancing near the bottom of the page, she saw something about adventure, but she had the picture of Marcia now well formed in her mind. She closed the book. It was a good sign to be born under she supposed, but it could not be compared with Sagittarius, to be sure.

June arrived bringing with it more adversity than Jo could recall of previous years. School was out. Marcia failed her grade again. The crops were dying in the fields for lack of rain. The weather was so hot, not a chicken could be seen in the yard. They stayed in the hen-house scratching for a cool place to squat. Jo hitched one of the mules to a two-wheeled cart and drove down to the lower end of the field where a small branch flowed across it from a creek that was a mile away. Contrary to her expectations, the branch still maintained a steady flow. Lou Ayers had seen her from the peanut field and followed her. No telling what this woman had on her mind, he mused as he approached her. "Lou" she yelled, with a hand on each hip. "There ought to be a way to keep all this water from going to waste." Lou pondered," How?" Jo glared at him," I didn't say I knew how. I said there ought to be a way, and there is if I can just figure it out." Lou drawled," I can't imagine how." Jo snapped, "Well, you wont be able to figure it out by this time next year either, but I will." She could barely tolerate the indolence in this man." In the meantime, there's only one thing to do. Hitch the other mule to the wagon, get those three barrels and meet me back at the well." Stunned, Lou protested. "Miss Marshall, we never will haul enough water to save our crops." "We'll never save any of them it we don't get started. Hurry!'

Thus the irrigation got under way with Jo and Marcia on the wagon with two barrels, and Maria and Lou on the cart with one. Water was hauled from daylight to dark. The vegetable garden had already lifted its head productively by the end of the week, when Jo again soaked it. Lou Ayers muttered and growled for the three weeks that Jo's irrigation was in process. Marcia worked without comment or complaint. Maria produced like a Trojan, wise-cracking with Jo. Jo was tired, both body and mind, but she was the only one who knew it. Maria learned to translate some of Lou's muttering sounds and understood him when she heard him say," Never again will I be fool enough to work for a damn woman." Maria took her stand. "You don't have to now. We can do just fine Mr. Ayers, with or without you." Lou looked at her, "What do you mean?" "I heard what you said, but I won't tell her. Just the same, you don't have to stay. We can do the work without you, or we can get someone else. Aunt Jo has already said that you have too much lead in your britches to suit her." "You better watch your mouth small fry, unless you want me to tell your aunt what you said." Maria laughed." I don't think you will, unless you want her to know what you said." She stuck her thumbs under the apron of her overalls and walked briskly past him to dip another bucket of water from the barrel. Lou heard a distant roar and looked upward. There were clouds forming with a threat of rain. Tomorrow was church day. "Let's call it a day," Jo said. "Looks like the Lord is promising us rain."

The rain did come during the night and lasted through the Sabbath. Jo could not attend the services that she seldom missed, but she was too grateful for the rain to complain. Instead, she got her Bible and summoned the girls to her. Sit down." she ordered." We'll have our own reading. No reason why we can't hear about the Lord right here in our home. We surely can't use the rain as an excuse for not worshiping. Opening the Bible, she began, "Train a child in the way he should go; and then when he is old, he will not depart from it." She turned a page, "Open thy mouth, judge righteously, and plead the cause of the poor and needy." "Aunt Jo, what are you reading?" Marcia wanted to know. Closing the book, Jo looked up," Proverbs." She said. And what are you reading?" Jo directed her question to Maria who was looking at some small book of her own. Maria replied, "Oh, it's just about things women should know." Jo inquired, "What kind of things?" "Little good you would have gotten from church today, if you had rather read than listen, then you read to me and Marcia from your book." Maria placed the book under her and said, "I can't." Jo held out her hand," Then give it to me."

Abruptly, Maria handed Jo the book, then reclaimed her seat. Jo read the book's cover. "Things women should know. She opened the book and was shocked speechless at the vivid diagram of what appeared to be a printed uterus. She turned the page, extremely disturbed viewing diagrams of the various stages of fetus development. Her eye mussels weakened; she could not look nor away, but stared unbelievingly at the diagrams. She attempted to speak, but her vocal cord had also weakened. Marcia started toward her." What is it, Aunt Jo?" Jo closed the book. Marcia glanced at her young sister whom she suspected to be the reader of dirty books. "Where did you get that awful book," Marcia demanded to know. "None of your business where I got the book. And it is not awful at all. It's about our bodies and how they function. How babies are conceived and grow before they are born" Marcia placed both her hands over her mouth. Turning around three times as if she had vertigo, she sat down. Jo still suffering from shock, had not yet recovered her speech and merely observed the behavior of the girls with a blank mind. "Aunt Jo, you should spank her good," Suggested Marcia who was now nervously cracking her knuckles. "Oh, for Pete's sake, it's about time we learned about the birds and bees. And being a human being, I want to know about people too. It's a good book. Mrs. Baggett said it was." Yelled Maria. "Mrs. Baggett, I don't believe it." Yelled Marcia. "Who cares what you believe?" Maria asked. "You should have been listening when Aunt Jo was reading Proverbs," Maria jumped up, got the Bible, "I'll read you something from Proverbs." She promised. "A wise man will hear, and will increase learning; and a man of understanding shall attain unto wise counsels. Turning a few pages she read on." If thou be wise, thou shall be wise thyself; but if thou scorns, thou shall bear it. A foolish woman is clamorous; she is simple, and knows nothing." Jo watched her as she tossed the book in her chair, and started toward the kitchen. "That girl's got spunk." Jo said to Marcia.

Doug Lawrence was a nice clean-cut boy of fine upbringing and family roots. He had polished manners that Jo was taking notice of. She liked the boy's outgoing personality; the way he shook hands and bowed to his elders at the church. He would make, she decided, a good match for Marcia who had not yet took notice of him. Maria had taken notice of him. Jo had seen the way she would hang around him on the church grounds teasing with him a bit too devilish. That one was too young however for any thoughts of match-making. Anyway, Jo wanted Maria to become a nurse, since that seemed to be her greatest interest. It was Marcia, who had already dropped out of school that Jo was concerned about right now. After they returned home from church, Jo said to Marcia," You know, the more I see of that Lawrence boy, the better I like him." Maria answered, "Me to." Jo looked at her. "You are not old enough to like boys yet. That boy is too old for you anyway. He is the age of Marcia. How do you like him, Marcia?" "He's very nice." She commented. Maria informed her "Well, you've got to wear your hair loose if you want him. He doesn't like braid." "And just how do you know that?" Jo asked. "Because he told me."

From the General store, Jo purchased some pretty fabric to make Sunday dresses for the girls. Because

Marcia's hair and eyes were brown, Jo thought yellow would make her more attractive. Though Maria would never need dressing up to draw attention from young men, Marcia's quiet, reserved nature demanded it. Marcia, she decided, must be made beautiful, but Maria was born with it. "Oh, Aunt Jo, this dress is lovely, but it would look better on me." Maria beamed. "You will do just fine with any color at all." Jo assured her as she assisted in arranging Marcia's hair. Doug Lawrence did take notice of Marcia. Not many people had ever seen her hair hanging around her shoulders. And as Jo had instructed Marcia, she took notice of Doug too. Soon Doug was getting invitations to Sunday dinner and was accepting them with enthusiasm. He enjoyed both of the girls; they were different enough to add a variety to his visits, not to mention the spice offered by Jo's straight forward manners. He knew exactly why Jo kept inviting him, and he found amusement in her endeavors. He had already developed an interest in Marcia which eliminated the necessity of Jo' efforts to bring them together. He liked Jo; she was easily read, and he admired her joviality attitude. He had been taught however, to have much respect for girls like Marcia who were quiet, well behaved, and never displaying too much gaiety. Her kind most always made trustworthy wives, and seldom, if ever, tried to boss their husbands. They made kind and understanding mothers. His own mother was such a woman as he now pictured Marcia to be. She was not beautiful nor brilliant, but homely and sweet. With this trend of thought, his pulse began to throb creating an emotional experience that he had not before enjoyed. It was during one of those crazy moments that he asked Marcia to be his wife. Marcia, having a pulse throbbing experience of her own, as he took her hand, agreed. Doug had walked Marcia home from the League and after exchanging "Good nights," he departed. Breathlessly, Marcia entered the house where she immediately but bashfully, announced her betrothal. Jo was dismayed. Though she had been gathering the fire wood, she had not yet intended to start the fire. "Get married! You and Doug. Has he kissed you?" Maria demanded to know. "Be quiet." Jo told her.

Marcia was indeed a lovely bride. As Maria kissed her, she whispered," You look like an angel." And she did to everyone, who filled the sanctuary to witness the nuptial rites. Her long white gown, made by Jo, settled around her feet with just enough seeded pearls not to rob the bride of her own beauty. Jo sniffed into her handkerchief as was expected of her, but betrayed her pretense by admiring the alter decorations that she herself had done. White and yellow mums with green lace fern, never had this little chapel been so well adorned. The reception was the biggest social event this community had known. Jo's tears were for real as she recalled other rites this chapel had held for her and the girls. She wished Sam and Eva could have been there. Maria caught the bride's bouquet of yellow mums. She hadn't wanted to do it, but Marcia tossed it to her. The other girls were jumping and climbing over the pews to catch the bouquet. Everyone kissed the bride, and all the ladies kissed the groom. Maria was troubled about whether she should kiss Doug. Having had no brother, she found difficulty in being sisterly to him.

Doug had been watching her, and she had noticed it. Even during the ceremony, he had cast a glance at her. After kissing her sister affectionately, she planted a kiss on Doug's cheek without putting a hand on him. "I always wanted a brother." She said. Doug put an arm around her holding her close to him. She whispered into his ear." But I didn't want him to be you."

Doug and Marcia moved into Jo's house that had been vacated by Lou Ayers, and had been redecorated for them. Doug was to take over management of the farm which Jo was confident he could handle. She had already learned his birthdates and that he was born under the sign Capricorn, the goat, and he was therefore some what of a go-getter himself. She had also found that the Capricorn was suited for matrimony with the Cancer. So in spite of an earlier wedding than she had hoped for, she was well content.

Maria avoided any encounters with Doug by visiting her sister only when she was sure that Doug was in the field. Though her visits were widely spaced, she observed that Marcia was a fair housekeeper and cook. From time to time however, she wondered if Marcia was performing her wifely duties as well. The thought of Marcia and Doug in a lovers embrace was tormenting to her soul. Yet, more than her own contentment, she wanted happiness for her sister and Doug. On one visit, she presented to Marcia the little book that Mrs. Baggett had given to her. "Here, you may find this book a little less dirty now. It contains information that you should know." Marcia's face flushed; she lowered her eyes looking at Maria's feet.

"I've already read it," Maria took the book home in disgust with her sister's shyness, and contempt for her secretive manner of reading the book.

The linoleum Jo ordered to cover her and Maria's floor arrived the very day that her arthritis was acting up. Her arms and shoulders were useless with pain. "Doug is coming to help me get it down, but I think you had better take my place, and let me just supervise." She told Maria who was giving her liniment rub-down. "Don't you worry, we'll get the floors finished, but the supervisor must stay in bed today." Maria spanked her aunt affectionately and made ready for the task of laying linoleum. With her jeans rolled up past her calves, she began moving the table and chairs from the kitchen. Doug knocked on the back door. "Come on in Doug," she yelled without any attempt to greet him. "Where in Aunt Jo?" he asked. "In bed with old age, but don't tell her I said so. We can put the rugs down without her, can't we?" Doug nodded his head. For a moment their eyes met and held; then Maria turned from him and began to unroll the linoleums. With his pocket knife, Doug trimmed the edges and corners to fit, as Maria sled around on her buttocks to smooth the linoleum to lay flat. As they had finished, Doug took her hands to pull her up from the floor. Having her on her feet, he placed both of her arms around himself and held them. They were thus embraced, when Jo entered the room and saw them. Having not been seen however, she immediately returned to her bed. When Doug had left, Maria went to check on her patient. Outside Jo's door, she knocked. "Come on in." Jo snapped." Why do you have to knock to enter my room?" Maria laughed," I didn't know if Arthur Ritus was still in bed with you." Maria kissed her aunt and laughed again. "Have you been asleep?" "Yes. You just woke me up." Jo lied. Maria took a bow," Your rugs have been laid madam. What else can I do for you?" Jo stared at her, "You sure are in a good spirit. You and Doug must have had fun working together. What did you two talk about?" "Mostly, we talked about linoleum." Maria started out of the room, then turned back." Aunt Jo , do you think Marcia and Doug are getting along well? Is Marcia doing all the things a wife should do." "I'm sure she is Maria, and their life is none of our business. So don't speak of it again. You understand?" Maria left the room.

Maria picked up an old quilt and went out doors to sit beneath the pecan trees. Doug had not kissed her, through no fault of his own however, for he had attempted to. She had turned her head to one side to avoid it. In his embrace, it suddenly came to her that he was her sister's husband. Jo tugged at her pillow trying to find comfort. She closed her eyes but sleep would not endow her. Visions of Maria in Doug's arms tortured her. She got out of bed and wandered idly to the window. Standing there, she spied Maria under the pecan trees. She was lying on her stomach with her elbows as props. Both of her feet were up in the air slowly swaying to and fro. Jo watched her for a while, then turned away. Poor child, she mused, we're both thinking about the same thing. In the kitchen, she heated up the left-overs and called Maria to come eat. They ate in silence, and in silence they both departed to their own rooms.

The rain came down in torrents; the wind howled a violent threat; and the class of twenty nine men and women were graduating. Jo had gone before noon to the school, as many others had done, to beat the rain. She sat now in the crowded auditorium straining her ears to hear the speaker of this great event. She wanted to see Maria receive her high school diploma. She searched through the crowds for a sight of Doug and Marcia. She wanted them to sit with her to share this eve of her ecstasy. That had been their plans, but she doubted now that they would come at all. The weather was bad. Marcia avoided getting wet when possible, and lacked the energy to have made an early start. Plans had been completed for Maria to leave soon after graduation to begin her nurse training. Both she and Jo were exultant over this education that they both long desired. Though the matter was never discussed, each of them looked forward to Maria's departure. Her leaving would surely release much tension in their household and alleviate their anxieties over Doug. "Maria Josephine Marshall" the principal yelled out, jolting Jo to her feet and bringing her back to the event at hand. Teary eyed now, Jo applauded with all her might as Maria took the rolled diploma into her own hands. "The prettiest girl on stage and no family except me to celebrate with you." Jo whispered to herself. Jo took Maria into her arms back stage and sobbed with her. You and I make a darn good family without anyone else." Maria comforted her. "I am so proud of you Aunt Jo. Without you I would have never got this far, but with you, there is no telling how far I will go." Jo beamed with gratitude, and as she whispered a prayer of thanks, Maria rushed into the arms of Doug who stood soaking wet in the doorway. "You can't come in here; some of the girls are still dressing." She guided him into the corridor. "How long have you been here?" she asked. "Long enough. I saw it all, but was too wet to take a seat. I stood in the hall and watched. You are beautiful." Maria was in his arms again when Jo approached them. "Oh, I see you did make it Doug. Where is Marcia?" Startled, he released Maria, except for her hand that he held tight, as he replied. "Marcia didn't feel well, and the weather was too rough for her to get out." Then to Maria he added, "It would have taken a snow storm in hell to have kept me from coming." He kissed her forehead, then with an arm around both ladies, he guided them out.

Jo saw two shadows through the paper shades that only partially protected the room's occupants. Why Maria didn't put the light out, was beyond her. Jo scolded herself for being a peeking-tom instead of leaving her spy post. She was too astonished to ignore what she was witnessing. Whether Doug had taken Maria into his arms, or if she had merely walked into them could not be determined from anyone who was not actually in the room. Jo concluded, however, that no force was being experienced by either. It was too obvious that those two were in mutual agreement. Wretchedly, she watched them until Maria removed her clothing. Doug removed his shirt. For a moment they stood embraced, pressing their naked bodies together. The light went out. Jo stood still and quiet except for her pulse beat that became faster and louder. Thinking now of Marcia, she went to check on her whereabouts. Marcia was soundly sleeping as Jo eased her door open to look in. "God, please don't let her ever know." She prayed.

Though Jo missed Maria, she avoided loneliness by taking care of Marcia. Doug's able management of the farm alleviated Jo's anxieties concerning the farm. It had been a good year, and the harvest would yield abundantly.

Maria was excited about going to college. She had always wanted to be a nurse. Maybe she and Doc could work together. At least they had the same interest. Maria wanted to help people. Nursing would be a good field to travel through. And there would be many who could benefit from her knowledge. She had a short time to get ready. Going to Atlanta thrilled her ego. She smiled as she decidedly whispered to herself." It's about time I flew out of the nest. I've been here long enough. There are bigger and better things for me. I just have to make sure my aim is always on the target. She would be the first one in the family to go to college. What puzzled her most was, where did Jo get the money to send her. Maybe she had more than Maria was aware. She knew Sam didn't have enough money to send her. They had lived one year at the time. Time came for her to leave. Doc came to see her off. He and Jo took her to the bus station. Doc put her luggage on the bus, and escorted her to her seat. Jo stood outside looking through the window at them and wiping tears that kept dripping down her face. Maria yelled at Jo, "I'll keep in touch." The bus took off. Doc took Jo into his arms "She will be back," he whispered.

Marcia gave birth to an eight pound daughter with no complications. Seeing Marcia care for her own baby gave Jo a warm feeling that she had seldom known. Jo, holding the infant close to her bosom, caressing its buttocks, as the kissed it's head, would elapse into a profound meditation. Tearfully, she would then place the child into its mother's arms. Jo had only a couple of times ever felt such strong attachment to a human being as she did to this tiny creature who had reached out and twined itself around her heart. She was almost in complete bliss as she held this baby. The only thoughts that shadowed her bliss were those of Eva and Sam. Marcia had proved herself a capable mother; marriage and child-bearing had forced her into a maturity more elevated than Jo had imagined Marcia had learned much from Doug, whom Jo deemed quiet shrewd, except for his escapade with Maria. Jo tried not to think about that, and if Doug gave thoughts to Maria, he never mentioned it. He was excited about his daughter and displayed nothing less than love and admiration for his wife. Jo felt no compunction for the marriage she had instigated. Doug had blundered; Doug was a man; Man is human: Humans blunder. Marcia did not know and could not hurt.

A letter from Maria explained her heavy work-load: endless hours of study would prevent her from coming home for Christmas. Hopefully, she would make it for Easter. Her family was gravely saddened at her absence during the holiday festivities. Maria had not come home last Christmas because of a research she was doing that required many hours of library work. Jo had much to do. She would move back into her own house, so that Marcia and Doug could come back home. They needed extra space now, and with all the additions Jo had added to the house, it really belonged to Marcia now. There was some sewing Jo had to do: A new dress for herself and Marcia, a new shirt for Doug, and best of all, a fine christening dress for Marcia Jo. The christening was the greatest event of the season. During the ritual Brother Nixon had made the mistake of announcing Jo as the baby's grandmother instead of godmother. Her eyes widened in surprise at the error, then with a warm feeling, she smiled at him. Marcia attempted to correct him, but seeing Jo's bliss, she did not. The congregation knew, but no one made comment. Mrs. Baggett brought her Kodak and made snapshots outside the church. Jo obtained copies of the pictures and sent them to Maria. "Please send them back to me." Jo wrote, "I never had my picture taken before." Maria returned the pictures with a framed enlargement for Jo. It was a picture of Jo holding the baby with Doug and Marcia standing on either side of her. Jo was delighted. This is the finest gift I ever received." She proclaimed. Maria sent other gifts: books for her sister, crib toys for her little niece, magazines for Doug, a sweater for Jo. She sent letters to Marcia encouraging her to read. With every letter came a pamphlet: 'How to be a good mother; Make yourself beautiful; Relax and feel well; Exercise. The lists went on and on. Marcia did read. It was a healthy two-mile walk to the mail box, and she went daily with great expectations. If the box was empty, as it usually was, she looked forward to tomorrow.

Jo had eaten her soup and was making ready to retire for the day, when she heard a faint knock on the kitchen door. "Doug, that you?" she called. It was Doug. "Something wrong Doug?" she asked. No, he only wanted to talk with her about a business deal. "Sit down Doug. What is it?" Doug sat down facing her. "I've spoken to Mr. Ashberry." Doug began. Jo stopped him. "My goodness Doug, you've talked with that young lawyer. I'm so proud of you. What on earth did you talk about? A lawyer, my goodness I don't think anybody in out family ever spoke to a lawyer. The only important people I know is Mrs. Baggett and Ole Doc Reeder." She hesitated, then went on "Tell me Doug, don't he own that big farm, the old Wight Place?" Doug was glad to finally have a chance to speak. "Yes. That's what I want to talk with you about. He wants to sell it, and I want to buy it." Jo let out a loud sigh," We don't have the money, Doug." Doug patted her on her shoulder. "I can make arrangements to get it. Five hundred acres!" Jo was speechless." I have enough money to make a deal. He has offered me a good deal. He will take much less than the land is worth because he is moving to Atlanta to practice law. His grandfather bequeathed him the place, and he says it's like a rope around his neck." Jo was angry." Guess all he cares about is money and law. But if you can get it, go ahead ,but be careful." She said. "I've heard that lawyers are cheats." Doug smiled amused. He was glad he had Jo's approval, since he had already signed the deed and a promissory note. Jo pondered the matter long after Doug had gone home. Guess all Doug cares about is family and land. "Mine and Sam's hundred acres is not big enough for Doug. Times have surely changed. She kept thinking to herself. Three generations of Marshall's made a living there and raised their families . Jo mused that Maria was still a Marshall. She would come home one day to live. "I will give her my house and fifty acres." She said aloud. Maria would come home and take care of the sick. She would be better than Ole Doc had ever been. That was exactly the reason Maria hadn't been home. She had stayed and studied her books. She would learn everything the books offered. She was smart. Marcia will probably be moving to the old Wight place. The house there was too big for one family to live in, lest they had a dozen or more siblings. Marcia had been a bit short winded lately as though she was in the family-way again.

Jo wanted to see Maria. She had not been able to come home for Easter. Making preparations for her graduation in June, had kept her too busy for the long planed visit. Jo missed Maria and wanted, more than ever, to sit down and talk with her. At letter writing, Jo was a procrastinator. Letters never allowed one to ask questions and give immediate answers, if indeed any answers at all. Maria never answered questions: she never gave much information concerning herself. Her letters were merely filled with news of her schedules, instructors, nursing duties, and lectures, none of which Jo could understand or appreciate. She had written Maria that Doug and Marcia had bought the Wight farm and had moved to it. Jo pondered Maria's indifferences. Surely she had outgrown her fling with Doug. Jo had hoped Maria would marry some young doctor, but not for some years yet. Maria was a nurse and should spend time enjoying her career before marriage. She prayed that Maria would not be an old maid like herself.

Jo assisted Doug and Marcia in their moving. She had cared for little Maria Jo, and had enjoyed doing it. The baby was looking more like Eva as she grew older. Marcia was heavy with child and would deliver in the fall. Both Marcia and Doug appeared very excited about the forthcoming baby. Contented now about Marcia and Doug because of the love and adoration they displayed for each other, and because of their unquestionable happiness, Jo began to worry about Maria. Marcia had achieved a happiness, a lofty peak of contentment, a fulfillment of womanhood that Maria and herself had not.

Sitting over a hot cup of coffee at her dinning table, Jo wrote a brief note to Maria before retiring to bed.

> *"Dear Maria,*
>
> *Please come to see us. I never meant for you to become too educated for your own family. We still love you. Little Maria Jo is walking now. She is very precious and looks like Eva. You should come to see her as well as your sister. I know you still love us, but let us know it."*
>
> *Love and Prayers,*
>
> *Aunt Jo*

Jo put the note in an envelope and went to bed. She prayed; she cried; she meditated. What was wrong with Maria? Was it because of Doug that she had not come home. Had she met a young man who demanded her free time. Maria had never mentioned a man, but surely she knew at least one. What kind of life was she living in the big city. Was sending her away to college a mistake. Jo asked herself many questions, but she had no answers. In September, Marcia gave birth to her second daughter. She and Doug had both wanted a son, but Marcia was not too disappointed. Doug was almost crushed at the news of another girl. He needed to raise a good farm hand. Jo took over Marcia's chores carrying for her house and family, and had little time to dwell on thoughts of Maria.

> *"Dear Aunt Jo, since my graduation last summer, I have been working at the hospital full time, but I will be coming home in December, probably before Christmas, and may decide to stay. Because of you ,I am a good nurse, and you shall be nursed. I will not be alone, my son will be with me. You will love him and enjoy him. He looks like you, Marcia and his two little cousins. He is excited over meeting you and seeing his mother's home. He is your oldest grandchild, and he will be the man of your house.*
>
> *Love,*
>
> *Maria and Jody."*

Tearfully, Jo read her short letter over and over again. She felt a warm sensation throughout her body engulfing her with quiet serenity. The letter was too point-blank, but so was Maria. Yet, she thought the letter was shrouded with clouds too heavy to see through. Maria has a son! More than five years since Maria had been home, and now she's coming with a son, the oldest grandchild! Jody was almost five years old! Jo cried because she had not been with Maria when the child was born, as she had been with Marcia during her deliveries. She cried because of the heartaches Maria must have suffered. She cried because she did not know. Maria's letters had been cheerful enough filled with hospital news and bliss. "That girl's got spunk." Jo said to herself. "She's strong, determined, and sets her own sail. She's the captain and the crew." Jo put the letter in her pocket wondering if Maria had also broken the news to Marcia. Maria didn't mention Doug. She had never mentioned Doug. Doug! Doug! My God, No, no, no. Jo sat down and wept. Had she just penetrated the cloud? Jo became angry. She blamed Doug, then changed her mind. It was no more Doug's fault than Maria's. Maybe it was her fault for watching the event instead of stopping it. She could have, but she didn't. If she had however, it would have become a family bomb. All she could do now was to keep her mouth shut, and try not to think about it. She would never tell anyone. No. not even Doc.

Christmas was just three weeks away. Many things had to be done. Jo would re-open Sam's house. It belonged to Maria and Jody now. She would dust and clean: she would again 'Deck the Halls with Holly'. She must talk to Marcia and Doug and tell them to ask no questions. Maria's life was her own business. She and Jody must be warmly accepted. Jody was, after all a legitimate family member. A Marshall had given birth to him. Who cared that his father was a young doctor? Yes, Jo would tell them that. She would tell them that Maria had written about a certain single doctor, and she would dare them to ever mention it. They would believe her and Doug could stop wondering about it. Jo, in her heart, knew the truth, but she would never tell it. She had not always been a angel herself, but her past was far behind her. She didn't dwell upon it.

Jo met the bus. Maria and Jody came running to her. Jo had never been more excited. To see Maria again was like seeing a rainbow in the sky, shining, glittering, colorful, and spirit lifting. She was too excited. She held Maria in her arms a bit too long. Jody asked, "Mom when is she going to turn you loose?" Maria laughed, and Jo grabbed Jody. "Your turn young man." "Well, hello. How are you?" Maria laughed and took a step behind Jo. Jo turned her head. There stood Doc. He hugged Maria and shook Jody's hand."Good to see you." Jody looked up and asked, "Are you Doc?" Doc finally found his voice and answered."That's right." Doc took them home wondering,"How did this boy know him?"

Christmas was the greatest ever. The feasts and festivities were centered around Sam's house where Jo, Maria and Jody stayed. The little ones sang, danced laughed, and shared. Everyone, particularly Jo, was mesmerized by the stories Jody would tell . He was a big-city boy, and his tales were exciting and refreshing to the others. He had been to Atlanta Zoo, Stone Mountain, the Agarama, and to a battlefield. He talked of parks and play-grounds and Peachtree Street. He had shopped in some large stores, and spoke of several toys and books. He spoke of hospitals, doctors and nurses. Marcia and Jo were astonished at the boy's broad knowledge and at his superb manners. Though Marcia often blushed and put her hands to her face in embarrassment, she was envious of Jody's advancement. Jo, after covering her initial shock, spent much time listening to and questioning the lad. That boy had been taught, she mused. Marcia fell in love with her blue-eyed nephew. She felt sure that he had been sired by a famous doctor. She deemed him to be smarter that any other family member. Doug avoided Jody, as well as Maria, whenever possible. The boy looked too much like his mother to suit Doug. Though Doug did scrutinize Jody very closely observing his physical features, his mannerism, and his characteristic gestures, occasionally recognizing some of his own traits in the boy. He could not find the assurance he was seeking.

As Jo and Maria began to settle down for the night, Maria made each of them a cup of hot cocoa. "I was about to go to bed girl, I'm a bit tired." Jo moaned. "Not yet," Maria answered. "We have a matter to talk about." Jo looked at her but remained speechless. Maria began: "You know that my son calls you Granny, and though you never mentioned it to me, you know that he is your grandson. I have known for several years that you are my mother. It's been too obvious. I understand that a single woman in your day could not disgrace her family by having a baby. That's not true today. There is absolutely no way I would have given Jody to Marcia and Doug. I also know of course, that Marcia is not my sister, but my cousin. I'm sure she doesn't know that, and I will never tell her. I want you to know one thing. You have shown more love and affection for me than anyone else ever did. I always loved you for the love you showed me. And it's not because I was the youngest, it's something far more than that. It's something more profound, more genuine. I felt it, and I know it. I need you to confirm it. I need my real mother. I'm a big girl now, and need truth." Jo wiped tears from her own face, and stated: "Well, the truth is out, and no one ever told you. You're a smart girl to have figured it out for yourself. Sam, Eva, and myself took an oath never to tell you nor anybody else, and we didn't." The two women dried their faces and went to bed.

Maria wanted to know more. She needed more information.. Was Doc her Dad? If so, why didn't he marry Jo, or was he already married at that time? She knew Doc had been married, but didn't know what happened. Before she went to sleep, she visualized a list of questions she would ask while on her visit. She wanted the truth, the whole truth, and she would get it.

Winter eased into spring ,a time for toiling the soil and planting seeds. Doug was too involved in the enticement of the land to ponder over the mystery of Jody's paternal parent. He knew that the child had been born about nine months from the night of his frivolous affair with Maria. He, unlike his naïve wife, knew that Maria had not gone to Atlanta, where she knew no one, and entered into an affair as a freshman nursing student. Maria was not a person to be completely swept off her feet by a mere acquaintance. And woe upon the man who ever tried to rape her. Doug concluded that Jody was his son, and he would waste no more sleep contemplating the matter. He felt sorrowful for the hardships Maria must have endured. He felt sorrowful that he had not know, ad that Maria could not tell him. He could have, and would have, helped her had he known.

By March fifteenth, Doug had his seed into the ground. He had worked from dawn to dark, and he was on schedule .Jo worried about Doug. He was getting too thin. Hard work did not cause a healthy man to loose weight as Doug had. Jo had compassion for the man. He, too, had been worrying about the endless questions he surely had been asking himself. Surely Doug knew, and Jo knew, but she could not offer any comfort to him because neither he not Maria had any idea that she knew. Jo didn't believe in discussing personal matters. Again, Jo thanked God that Marcia did not know.

Jody had boasted that his daddy was a pilot. He had shown two pictures of a very handsome uniformed man standing by a large jet plane. Jody said the man was his father who was killed in a crash. No one questioned it, except the girls. They asked a number of questions, and Jody gave answers. Marcia had noticed that her husband did not sleep well; he nibbled at his food and did not eat well. He was loosing weight, he was very nervous, but she did not wonder too much about it. He had pushed himself hard to get the crops planted on time. The children kept her too busy to worry about things that did not demand her attention. Unlike the others, Marcia did not pursue self punishment. She slept well, ate well, and lived in sublime peace. Jo spoke to Maria," You looked a bit pallid child, are you sleeping well and felling well?" Maria laughed. "My dear ole aunty, I do not look pallid, and not ill in ay sense. Because you and Doug are trying to waste away, you think that I should. You are not eating and sleeping well yourself. Many days you stay in bed with arthritis when I know that it is not bothering you. You can't fool your nurse, you know. Do you want to talk about what's bothering you?" "I don't know." Jo lied. Maria smiled at her, "Well I know. You are asking questions to yourself about Jody, and you cannot supply the answers. You silly thing. When you want information, you must ask questions to someone who knows the answers. We have not talked about Jody's father, and it bothers you. I never questioned you about your hidden secret, and everybody knows that old maids know more than they tell. No, I am not sick anymore; I've had time to get well. Maria tried hard to hold back her own tears. She went to Jo again, knelt down, and put her arms around her. "Stop fretting, my darling mother. You have more reasons to be happy than to be sad. Your daughter finally acknowledges you in the only way that she ever could. She taught her son to call you Granny, a title that you so graciously deserve. Jo sobbed passionately in her daughter's arms. "It's time to rejoice and be happy." Maria declared. "I will ask you no more questions, and you will ask me no more. A mother and daughter do not have to stand naked before each other. I do want you to know, however, that I have forgiven myself, and God has forgiven me. I never held anything against you to forgive. Remember the Samaritan woman? She had had several husbands and lovers, but God forgave her and told her to go and sin no more. Can't you just see us now, dancing around His throne?" Maria pulled Jo to her feet, and the two women were standing embraced as Jody entered the room.

Jody began screaming. Granny! Granny! Aunt Marcia wants you. It's Uncle Doug. He's dead I think. Mother, you had better come too." The three of them ran in the direction the direction that Jody led them. "Save him! Help him! Do something!" Marcia pleaded with her sister. "There is nothing that I can do." Maria replied. "You're a nurse, aren't you?" Maria whispered. "I am not God." It was an ugly mess, Doug lying face up in a pool of blood beneath his tractor. His upper torso was crushed, and even his pores seemed to be spurting blood. It was too late to save him. Marcia fell to the ground and Jo grabbed her. Maria stood numb. She would not move; she could not speak; she could not cry. Jo was embracing Marcia, trying to get her off the ground. Maria saw the men who came; she heard their mummer. Someone took the women and children to Doug's house. Someone made coffee. There was food, people eating, laughing, crying, praying and fainting. People were going and coming, but Maria sat in a chair and looked without seeing. Someone took her hand and led her to bed, then pulled a light blanket over her. Then someone whispered to her to get up and get dressed for the funeral. At the funeral Maria sat solemnly staring at the casket that held Doug's body. She noticed the flowers. She noticed Jo trying to comfort Marcia ad her daughters. She saw Jody crying and attempting to comfort his cousins, but she heard not a word that was being said. The people all around her were crying; Maria heard not a sound. Her secret was sealed.

Marcia and her daughters spent the following week with Jo, Maria and Jody. "Oh, what will I do without Doug?" Marcia moaned. Jo thought Marcia would, without a doubt, moan forever. Maria went to her sister, took her into her arms, and said, "Marcia, I am so sorry for all that has happened, but death is never the end of life. As Paul wrote to the Corinthians. That is why we never give up. Though our bodies are dying, our inner strength in the Lord is growing every day. These troubles and sufferings of ours are, after all, quiet small and won't last very long. Yet this short time of distress will result in God's richest blessings upon us forever and ever. So we do not look at what we can see right now, the troubles are all around us, but we look forward to the joy in heaven which we have not yet seen. The troubles will past, but the joys to come will last forever in heaven." Maybe that would stop Marcia from feeling so sorry for her self, Maria thought.

All was well until they learned to love Jody. Doug had insisted that the will include Jody as an heir. Marcia agreed. She had wanted to include her sister's fatherless child. He might need someone to help him someday. Jo made no comments. Marcia further shared with them that Doug had migrating insurance to finish paying off the farm, and life insurance for her and the children. "Maria, Doug left one hundred acres to Jody." Maria was startled, "Why? For God's sake, why?" Marcia smiled "Because I love you, my only sister. Since Jody had no father to help him, I wanted him to be counted as one of our heirs. I love you and your son, that much." Maria ran to her sister crying. "O, Marcia, you should not have, but it's so sweet of you. I do love you and your daughters very much. I will always do whatever I can for you."

When the sisters had quit hugging, crying and kissing, Marcia turned to Jo who was smiling in world-filled bliss." Aunt Jo, what are we going to do about the farm now?' Before Jo could answer, Jody burst into the room. "Granny, I'm hungry." Jo took him to the table and fixed him a peanut butter and jelly sandwich. Then she turned her attention back to Marcia "Don't you worry about that darling. The three of us together can take care of anything. Marcia began crying again. "I don't know what to do. I don't have anybody to take care of me. Doug made all the important decisions. Without him, I'm lost."

Maria looked at Marcia disgustingly. After all, she had certainly pulled herself through some trying times. To find out that she was pregnant right after entering college was a great burden for her. She finished her first year just before Jody was born. She displayed a potbelly and was laughed at, whispered about, and given evil glances. She endured snickering from some of the boys. Many would ask, "Where is your husband?" She would always answer, "In the Air Force."Jody was born before her first summer break. She was terrified.What would she do? She surely could not let her family know, even though she needed some extended support. The hospital where she worked part time had a nursery for employees. Maria had taken advantage of that. She worked two shifts all summer. When fall came, she scheduled her courses for morning classes, worked forty hours a week, kept her grades up, took time for her son, and graduated.

Yes, she had some help from some friends, but her load was extremely heavy. She glanced at Marcia and angrily pondered. Which was worse, to lose your husband, or to never have one. Marcia had everything she needed, except Doug. She had enough money to support her household. They would never be in need. Her girls had lost their father: Jody never had one.

Jody entered the room."Granny, Mother said you are having a birthday in a month. How old will you be?" Jo smiled and replied. "Old enough to know what I want to do. And old enough to do it." Jody looked puzzled. "I have to ask my mother if I can do anything." Jo smiled. "When you get as old as I am, you wont have to." Jody looked at his mother, then said, "Mother said you are having a birthday party in a month. Maria laughed, "You were not supposed to tell her." Jody stalked toward the door, glanced at Jo and said." See what I mean?" All three of the women laughed. Jo thanked God

Many people from the church came to Jo's party. Marcia and Maria were so pleased. Many nice gifts were given to Jo, and the girls had prepared enough finger foods. As events began to fade, the crowd began to leave. Marcia and her girls had gone home with some friends for the rest of the evening.

All was gone but Doc Reeder. On his way out, he put an arm around Maria and held her close for a few minutes. She was quiet surprised. Then her brain began to ramble. Oh my God she thought. Is Doc my biological father? Yes. Of course he is. Why hadn't I suspected that before now? Doc said,"Maria you certainly have a handsome son. He is smart and well behaved too." He kissed her on her cheek, and started to leave. "Just a minute Doc." Maria pleaded. Jo was leering at her wide-eyed and in great wonderment. Maria put her arm around Doc. "Since my son calls Aunt Jo Granny, should he be calling you Grand daddy. I already know who my mother is. I would be so happy to know who my father is. And I think it's you. Am I right"? She glanced at Doc and Jo. They both put their arms around her, and together they said "Yes."

As Doc started out, he put his arms around Jody, pulled him close into his arms, kissed him on the forehead, "I know you want to go fishing. I'll pick you up at seven tomorrow morning. I need somebody to help me manage the boat." Jody was so happy, he almost screamed, "I'll be ready Grand Paw."

Maria fell to the floor on her knees. "Thank you God, My parents are still living, and my son has grandparents."

As soon as Doc left, Jo asked Maria, "How did you figure that out?" Maria placed both arms around Jo and explained "You always drew me close to you. You always whispered how much you loved me. No one else ever did. You spent a lot of time with me since I was a kid. There was always a warm feeling between us that I never felt with anyone else. There was also a special feeling between me and Doc. He would always pat me on the head or shoulder, tell me how pretty I was, and say very softly that he loved me. Doc gave me a special notice at church that he didn't give the other girls. That's where I was around him the most. So I've been adding two and two together for a long time, but only recently came up with four. Since Jody and I came home, Doc has spent much time with us, and has given Jody much attention. By the way is Doc the one who paid my college expenses?" After a moment, Jo replied, "Yes."

"Tell me about you and Dad, Why didn't you get married?" Jo was silent for a while. "Because he was already married." Jo uttered. "Go ahead." Maria pushed her. Finally, Jo told her. "I never loved anyone but Doc. He was married when I met him. I worked with him, fell in love with him, and got pregnant. You know how that goes." Maria caught the blow surprisingly, but let it go. "What about after his wife died?" Jo thought, then replied. "She has only been dead a few years." Maria glared at her "So?"

Jo explained," I worked with Doc after school. I was his secretary during my senior year. After I finished school, I went to work for Doc full time. At that time he was the only Doctor in this area. He delivered most all the babies, and treated most of the children. He was well known. and he was good. People liked him, and trusted him. He was most appreciated for his ability to put children back into school shortly after colds, flu, measles, chicken pox, and any thing else. Doc went into the homes of people who needed him. Very few people had phones out in this area. Most people came to the office to report a need in their homes. Doc would go, and I would stay in the office and wait for the next call. Doc paid me well. He picked me up every morning. and brought me home every evening. He showed me a gratitude that few people ever did. He was respectable, polite, and never failed to display great appreciation."

"I certainly see those qualities in Doc." Maria began."I have known him all my life, and have always liked him. I remember all the kids at church liked him. He would play with us, pick at us, and laughed a lot. I don't recall much about his wife. In fact, I vaguely remember her. Was she somewhat inactive? Did they not have any children of their own? " Jo was quiet for a while. "No. They had no children. His wife was, for some reason, not able to get pregnant. She didn't like to be around other people. I don't think she actually liked anybody. Not even Doc. The two years I worked for him, she never once came into the office. The only time I ever saw her was at church. She did not socialize or speak to anyone. Some thought she felt herself better than others, but I don't think so. She had some kind of problem. I don't think Doc knew either." Maria jumped up, stretched her arms above her head, ran her fingers through her hair, and said "It's kitchen time."

Sipping on hot cocoa, Maria asked, "Why didn't you and Doc get married after his wife died?" Ho laughed, "How much longer is this conversation going to last?" Maria smiled at her. "When ever you wish, but there are a few more things I need to know. She got up, kissed Jo, and said "You can not imagine how much I have enjoyed this mother-daughter talk."

Doc picked up Jody early, but he was ready. Jody had never been fishing, but his plan was to catch a boat full. When they arrived home late that evening, Jody was so excited he could barely talk. He told Maria and Jo all the surprised of the day. Doc caught five fish. Jody caught six. Maria had never seen her son so happy. She placed both arms around Doc."I love you Dad." Then, with both arms around her, Doc proclaimed, " I love you too. And I really love my grandson." Doc and Jody cleaned the fish and turned them over to the cooks. Maria called Marcia and invited her and the girls for dinner. The seven had a great meal together.

Both Jo and Maria had noticed some strange behavior in Marcia. They had been keeping the girls in late evening a bit too often. Marcia was supposed to be rearranging things in her house. Maria and Jo wondered why the girls could not help her. Or why didn't she ask them to help? Was she sneaking around seeing a man? Maria almost jumped out of her chair. Had Doug been gone a year yet? Did it matter? Marcia's business was none of hers. Who? When? Where? She couldn't turn her thinking power off.

After Doc left, Marcia announced that she was getting married in about a month. Jo and Marcia both knew Andrew. He and Marcia had grown up together through school and church. His family was very devoted to the church and was well known throughout the community. Jo had noticed some connection between Marcia and Andrew, but marriage? She was shocked. Marcia looked at Jo and Maria," Speaking of marriage, I think it's about time the other two single women got married." Jo was speechless. Maria agreed. Jody burst into the room, "Granny, how old are you?' Jo cleared her throat, "twenty years older than your mother." Jody pondered that for a while, then declared, "You are forty four." Jo smiled at him and said "Smart boy."Marcia began laughing. "See what I mean?"

Marcia and Andrew Carter were married at the church. A large crowd attended. Marcia's daughters both served as bride maids. Andrew's son was the best man. Following the reception, the Carters left for a honeymoon trip to New Orleans leaving the three children Jo and Maria. Jo was a upset that those arrangements had not been previously announced. Maria was very pleased to take care of the three. Jody was most excited to have all the cousins together. Jody was most pleased to have another boy in the family. Jo complained, "We are about to lose Marcia and the girls. They will probably move to New Orleans where Andrew's father has a law practice. Then there will be only three of us." Doc laugher. "No matter what the Carters do, they will still be family. Marcia will never be too far away, nor for too long a time." Maria hugged Doc and whispered, "Why don't you and Mom get married? Please do." Doc kissed her cheeks and softly whispered back, "We will."

Doc pulled Jody's ear. "Would you boys like to go for a boat ride?" Jumping up and down, both boys said "Yes." Maria asked "Dad, could the girls go too? They never get to go out on a boat." Doc laughed. "Of course they can go. It would be more fun with the girls." As soon as they were out the door, Jo sneered at Maria."What was that for?" Maria kissed Jo. "Remember we have some more things to talk about, and we need some privacy." Jo said, "Before we talk, let's have some peach pie."

As soon as they had eaten, Jo asked, "What is it you wish for now?" Maria took the dishes off the table, poured two glasses of tea, and sat down. She began. "I don't remember my grandmother. I have wondered why you didn't keep me. You had your mother who could have helped you. Did she worry too much about what people would say about a single pregnant girl? If that was her problem, then it was a great one. I can't imagine ever giving my child to someone else. I went through a lot of harassment myself, but I struggled through it, and kept my baby. A baby is a great part of it's Mother. I know you didn't have the choices I had, but why?" Jo was silent for a while. She sipped her tea, looked around the room confirming that the two of them were alone. Then she began. "I was sent to live with my grandmother. My mother made arrangements with Eva and Sam to take the baby. She wanted to keep it in the family. My mother and Doc were the only ones who knew of my condition. Doc paid my grandmother to care for me. He always supported you. He always loved you. As soon as his wife died, he asked me to marry him. I refused. Now, that's enough. "No. No. Why did you refuse?" Jo was a bit upset. "Because, I always blamed him for my pregnancy. He should have known better." Maria burst into laughter. "Did he rape you?" "No, he didn't." Jo yelled. Marcia was laughing a bit too much to please Jo. "Why blame him? It takes two to tango." Jo left the room and went out on the porch. Maria followed her. She placed her arms around Jo, and began to pray. After she had finished, Jo prayed. Maria then announced ,"We do not have to speak of this again. I just needed to know. More than anything else, I am so grateful that Jesus forgives, and He has forgiven both of us. He has so graciously blessed me, and I am free. What other people say or think about me, is not my problem. It's theirs."

Doc brought the children home before dark. They did not fish. They went all over the lake, took their shoes off and waded in the shallow edges. They took a hike in the woods, and saw many flowers and trees that awed them. They were excited about different birds they saw. They all sat on the porch together and listened as each of the kids talked and dramatized different experiences of the day. "It was a great trip." Doc proclaimed. Maria thanked Doc for all he had done. She gave him a big hug before he left. Jo also expressed her appreciation to Doc. "Mom, can I go home with Grand Paw." Jody wanted to know. "No. He needs a break." Doc waved good-bye, and took off smiling.

Jo and Maria made a list of things to do before Easter. They cleaned the Marshall house for Marcia and her family to come home to. Marcia had expressed her desire to move back into the house. Jo had wondered why. Her house on the farm was much larger. Maybe too many memories of Doug still lingered there. Jo arranged to add two more rooms to Sam's house. She had the house painted, and along front porch was added. She then did the same thing to her house. When all the work was finished, Jo gave Marcia and Maria each a house with one hundred acres. She gave each one of them a deed. They were very pleased.

Marcia noticed Jo and Doc in the back yard talking and pointing in all directions. What in the world were they doing? She soon found out. Doc began building a large square building outback of Maria's house. "What are you doing?" She asked Doc. His reply was, "Getting ready for Easter." He had concrete flooring, several long tables and benches, several windows, and a rest room, In one corner was a small kitchen. Now Maria approached Doc."Why?" He threw a small rock at her, without hitting her, and answered. " It's for family reunions, come rain or come shine." Maria looked around and suggested, "Maybe we should put three or four single beds or cots next to the wall, for those who might get tired and would like to relax." Doc looked around a bit surprised, then said, "Sounds good to me. You do it." Maria quickly replied, "O.K. I will."

Maria was a bit disturbed. There seemed to be something going on that she did not know. Doc was doing too much work there on her place. He had Jody helping him to pick up this, or go get that. Jody was happy to work with Doc. Jody loved him, and looked somewhat like him. Did they really need that huge picnic building? Did Jo need to do all the work she had done?

Easter was only a month away. Marcia and Marcia needed to do some shopping. Andrew took the ladies into town. Jo kept the four children. As they shopped, they began to share some concerns. Marcia asked Maria had she noticed anything strange about Jo. Maria thought for a moment and said, "Yes ,I have been aware of it for a while." Marcia added, "I noticed it as soon as I came back home. And I have wondered why Aunt Jo added those rooms to the houses, and why did she give us the deed. Do you suppose she is sick, but not going to tell us?" Maria pondered that a few seconds. "No. She is not sick. I believe she and Doc are going to get married .But don't you tell her I said that." Marcia quickly responded, "I have thought that too. Doc is here a lot more since Daddy died. He never came around much before that. Maria, I have another question. Why do you call Aunt Jo Mom?" Maria laughed."I know it sounds silly, but I want Jody to have a Granny. He knows that would be my Mother." Marcia laughed. "I think I'll ask my girls to call her Granny. It will be a closer family connection." She laughed and continued. "If Aunt Jo, I mean Mom and Doc get married, my girls can call him Grand Paw like Jody does." Maria added to that, "So can Bishop. Why not?" They both laughed. "I will have to talk to Andrew about that."

Just before they headed for home, Marcia said, "I have one more thing to share with you, but it's a secret until you hear it from someone else." Amazed, Maria said "Spill your beans darling, That's what sisters are for." Marcia began. "Andrew doesn't want us to keep the farm. He has never lived on a farm, and has no interest in it. I don't want to go back there either. I have sold the farm to Doc, but he told me to keep quiet about it. I thought you should know."

Easter morning Doc came by to pick up Jo, Maria, and Jody. When they arrived at the church, Andrew, Marcia, and their three were waiting for them. When the service ended, the pastor asked everyone to remain in their seats. More was to come. To every ones surprise, the pastor yelled out loud. "Doc Reeder and Jo Marshall, step forward." They did. As soon as each of them had said "I do," the whole Marshall clan surrounded them.

Several friends went home with them carrying food. The picnic shelter was large enough for all to enter into. There were plenty of tables and benches. Maria couldn't eat for laughing and crying. She announced to the crowd that she had never been happier. Jo and Doc went to her. The three embraced.

"Thank you Lord," Maria screamed.

About the Author

Eunice Long is a strong woman. She has been up the mountains and down in the valleys. Through her determination, fueled by positive views, she has achieved her goals. Raised on a farm, she learned to get the work done. As a college graduate, she directed a writing lab. As a mother, she taught her two children the way to go, and they never veered too far from the path. The most important issues in her life have always been her family.

Eunice shows her readers a rainbow attitude by showing them that any problem can be resolved in a loving and caring family. Without great relationships with family, life in this world has little value.

What Eunice values most, is that she and her family are Christians.